New York's Financial Markets

Conservation of Human Resources
Studies in the New Economy

New York's Financial Markets: The Challenges of Globalization, edited by Thierry Noyelle

Immigrant and Native Workers: Contrasts and Competition, Thomas R. Bailey

Beyond Industrial Dualism: Market and Job Segmentation in the New Economy, Thierry J. Noyelle

Computerization and the Transformation of Employment: Government, Hospitals, and Universities, Thomas M. Stanback, Jr.

Technology and Employment: Concepts and Clarifications, Eli Ginzberg, Thierry J. Noyelle, and Thomas M. Stanback, Jr.

New York's Financial Markets

The Challenges of Globalization

EDITED BY

Thierry Noyelle

Columbia University

Routledge
Taylor & Francis Group

LONDON AND NEW YORK

First published 1989 by Westview Press, Inc.

Published 2018 by Routledge
52 Vanderbilt Avenue, New York, NY 10017
2 Park Square, Milton Park, Abingdon, Oxon OX14 4RN

Routledge is an imprint of the Taylor & Francis Group, an informa business

Copyright © 1989 by the Conservation of Human Resources Project, Columbia University, and the New York State Urban Development Corporation

Library of Congress Cataloging-in-Publication Data
New York's financial markets : the challenges of globalization/
   edited by Thierry Noyelle.
      p. cm.—(Conservation of Human Resources studies in the new economy)
   Includes index.
   ISBN 0-8133-0832-1
   ISBN 0-8133-0833-X (pbk.)
   1. Financial institutions—New York (N.Y.) 2. Money market—New York (N.Y.) 3. Capital market—New York (N.Y.) I. Noyelle, Thierry J. II. Series.
HG184.N5N38 1989
332.1'09747'1—dc19   88-27784
                                                                 CIP

ISBN 13: 978-0-367-00338-8 (hbk)
ISBN 13: 978-0-367-15325-0 (pbk)

Contents

Tables and Figures

Figures

Acknowledgments

As the final touches are put to this book, I cannot but thank all of the contributors for their unusual kindness and exceptional assistance in preparing their chapters for the publisher on very short notice. I also want to thank Matthew Held of Westview Press, whose own excitement for this book guaranteed that it could be published in record time. I also wish to extend my gratitude to Ellen Levine and Shoshana Vasheetz. As always, they demonstrated great patience and skill in dealing with the unnerving process of endless revisions, corrections, and copy editing. Finally, I must express my very special thanks to Penny Peace, my associate at the Conservation of Human Resources Project, who took prime responsibility for overseeing the preparation of this book. Without her work, this book would not be quite the same.

This book was inspired by a seminar I organized on May 26, 1988, at the request of New York State Governor Mario Cuomo's Advisory Panel on Financial Services and Panel Chairman Vincent Tese, New York State Commissioner of Economic Development. I am most grateful to Rick McGahey and Mary Malloy at New York State's Department of Economic Development for their encouragement and support throughout the course of this project. Last but not least, I am most thankful to Laura Dillon and Pat Dempsey, at J. P. Morgan, for their hospitality and that of their institution, where the conference was held.

Points of views and opinions expressed in this book are solely those of the contributors and do not represent the positions or policies of either the Governor's Advisory Panel on Financial Services or New York State.

Thierry Noyelle

1

Overview:
Issues for the 1990s

Thierry Noyelle

Shortly after October 19, 1987, a long-time observer of the New York economy suggested that that day's market crash marked the end of the 1980s.[1] If October 19, 1987, does indeed represent such a benchmark, then the pickup in financial activity and renewed regulatory developments in the United States, in Europe, and among the central banks of the largest developed countries during the first half of 1988 suggest that the restructuring of financial industries will continue during the 1990s at a pace as furious as that of the 1980s.

Indeed, while 1987 saw retrenchment in corporate bond markets in both New York and London, a spate of new issues beginning in the first quarter of 1988 breathed new life into these two largest markets. Likewise, after barely a pause, mergers and acquisitions, leveraged buyouts, and related financial engineering gained new strength in New York in early 1988 and suddenly blossomed in Europe where such activities had remained quite limited in scope until then.

Perhaps more significant, June and July 1988 were witness to a series of regulatory developments, both here and abroad, which suggested that more churning was in the offing. Remarkably, on the very same day that the European Community's (EC) financial ministers approved a plan that would end all restrictions on capital movement within the twelve-nation trading block—namely, on June 13, 1988—the U.S. Supreme Court let stand a decision that gives commercial banks limited new authority to underwrite and deal in U.S. commercial paper, mortgage-backed securities, consumer loan-backed securities, and municipal revenue bonds.[2] Less than a month later, on July 11, 1988, the heads of the world's twelve largest central banks, including Japan, the United States, Switzerland, and the key EC countries, signed a final agreement setting more stringent and standardized capital requirements for international banks.[3]

Sensing that October 1987 hardly marked the end of the long period of intensive transformation characteristic of the 1980s, but rather marked the beginning of a new phase of change, a few weeks after the crash, New York State Governor Mario Cuomo called upon New York's financial industries to help his administration assess their sector's own future. The Governor's Advisory Panel on Financial Services was created in November 1987. A few weeks later, I had the privilege to be asked by the Panel to organize for May 1988 a one-day seminar focusing on the implications of the continuing globalization of financial markets for New York with a view to help the Panel map out some of the issues.

Thanks to the tremendous support and interest from the members of the Advisory Panel, and the very special assistance from J.P. Morgan which hosted the meeting, the seminar produced strong discussions among participants and raised very tough questions; so much so, that it seemed appropriate to bring together, in a book, a number of the themes that emerged there.

I believe this book is one of the very first ones to look beyond the 1980s and to address some of the critical issues that New York will need to confront in the early 1990s. In this respect, I hope that it will be a useful contribution to the policy debates that must take place among industry representatives and local, state and federal officials if New York is to retain its role as a leading world financial center.

Issues for the 1990s

Is the size of New York's capital markets likely to continue to shrink in the years ahead relative to London or Tokyo, even if the volume of local financial activity continues to grow in the absolute? Or, on the contrary, is New York so positioned today that it may enjoy faster rates of growth in the years ahead than its two principal competitors? If so, where do New York's future market opportunities lie?

Where will the challenges to New York come from in the future? As financial service industries enter a new phase of geographical decentralization, will the challenges come from London or Tokyo, as was the case during the 1980s; from Hong Kong and Singapore in Asia; from Paris, Frankfurt or Milan in Western Europe; or from Chicago, Los Angeles and Toronto in North America? Or will they come from New York's own inner weaknesses, including the difficulties encountered by its largest banks in mounting a successful counteroffensive to Japanese and European banks?

Finally, in the face of the continuing restructuring of the industry and its markets, what can public officials and regulators do to strengthen and prepare New York for the 1990s? These and others questions are addressed by the authors of the chapters presented in this collection.

In "International Stock Market Transactions," Roy Smith argues that international equity transactions, including cross-border transactions in secondary markets and new issues offered to investors under one of several different "globalized" distribution techniques, represent one area of financial activity where new growth can be expected and where New York should be well positioned to capture a large share of new business.

Smith reasons that New York, unlike London, is a relative latecomer to international financial transactions. The city, with its equity markets, stands at the center of the world's largest and perhaps most stable economy. Japanese and European investors are increasing their holdings in the United States and will continue to do so in the years ahead. Many U.S. companies still have no significant foreign stockholders; and many U.S. institutional investors have yet to make significant international equity transactions. Volume of new international issues and new activity in secondary markets will thus increase faster in New York than in London where the internationalization of the local markets is already more advanced. Furthermore, New York should be helped in the coming years by the fact that, relative to London or Tokyo, it has become a low-cost location, thanks in part to the dramatic exchange rate readjustments of the last two years—a theme explored also in several of the other chapters. Smith concludes with a note of caution, however, warning that the international financial community has become highly mobile and that New York will need to be attentive to adverse changes in taxation and regulation that could quickly undo the city's current advantage.

In "The Foreign Challenge to U.S. Commercial Banks," Robert Cohen is far more guarded in his assessment of New York's future. Implicit in Cohen's analysis is the notion that New York's strength as a world financial center will remain, in part, a function of the strength of U.S. commercial banks and securities firms. But this is where things have changed considerably during the 1980s, as the result of the successful challenge to U.S. dominance mounted by the leading European and, even more so, leading Japanese banks.

Of course, Cohen knows that in a world in which securities market activity has become dominant, traditional measures of asset size or market valuation may not be sufficient to compare competitiveness among major players. In his chapter, Cohen focuses on U.S. commercial banks and examines several measures of competitiveness, including not only traditional measures of "firepower" (assets and market value) but also indicators of "placing power," cost competitiveness, productivity, profitability, international market presence, and innovativeness. His findings are mixed. For, while measures of asset size and market valuation give the Japanese and leading European banks a growing advantage, other measures suggest that U.S. banks have retained competitive strength. In this respect, Cohen does discuss the implications of the new capital adequacy standards and of the shift from asset growth to profit growth for major groups of banks. While Cohen agrees that the shift of focus from assets to profits does present a challenge to Japanese banks, he does not think that the new capital adequacy requirements will be as big a challenge for them as some analysts have predicted.

Cohen concludes with a strong warning. In his opinion, the recent past suggests that Japan's Ministry of Finance (MoF) will promote the competitiveness of Japanese banks and their adaptation to the new market conditions (i.e., new capital adequacy requirements, the shift from asset growth to profit growth) in very much the same way that Japan's Ministry of International Trade and Industry (MITI) played a role in promoting the Japanese auto and semiconductor industries. Thus, in addition to developing the infrastructure and the policies that will further promote the city as a world financial center, New York State and City officials may need to take a lead in helping to develop institutional mechanisms that will enable U.S. banks to respond to a possible neo-mercantilist challenge.

The fact that the United States is no longer the undisputed economic, political, and financial power that it once was is, in Richard Levich and Ingo Walter's opinion, a factor that must form the basis of any analysis of New York's future as a world financial center. In "The Regulation of Global Financial Markets," Levich and Walter retrace the transformation of global financial markets. They identify those factors that help to explain the formation of major national and international financial centers in the past and those that will determine which, among them, will remain in the top league in the years ahead.

Focusing on the implications of the 1963 U.S. Interest Equalization Tax and later U.S. regulations that effectively closed foreign access to the U.S. bond market, thereby promoting the development of offshore markets out of London and Luxembourg, Levich and Walter argue that the daunting task for regulators is to design an "optimum" structure of regulation. Such a regulatory structure must provide a reasonable degree of prudence and stability at minimum cost to efficiency and financial innovation, while aligning policies among banking authorities internationally, so that no one market is at a competitive disadvantage. As Smith does in his chapter, the two authors recognize that the issue has become all the more pressing in that recent changes, including technological change and the relative decline of the United States, have contributed to making financial industries increasingly mobile.

Levich and Walter argue both that it is in New York's interest to ensure that the process of financial "deregulation" continues and that such a process is not inconsistent with the maintenance of a *positive* regulatory tax to protect the national financial system. In Levich and Walter's opinion, deregulation and a positive regulatory tax, combined with a push to truly open up both foreign and U.S. markets on the basis of "national treatment," should be the basis to define a new international level playing field in which New York stands a chance to preserve its role as a leading international financial center. But the road ahead is likely to be rugged and may require a much more proactive strategy on the part of state and local officials than has been historically the case.

The increasing mobility of financial industries and the challenge that such mobility represents for New York's future as a leading international financial center is also a central theme of my chapter. In "New York's Competitiveness," I try to identify and examine which forces of transformation—be they technological, market, regulatory, or public policy changes—may undermine or, on the contrary, strengthen New York's position. To do so, I review eight dimensions of New York's current competitiveness, including its traditional role as a magnet to issuers, investors, and financial intermediaries, its strength as a center of financial innovation, its technological infrastructure, its human resources, its operating cost environment, and its exceptional infrastructure of business support services.

A principal conclusion of my analysis is that New York is emerging from a phase in which international financial activity moved further away from New York, toward Tokyo, and even more so, toward London, but during which national financial activity became increasingly concentrated in New York. It is now entering a new phase. In this phase, New York may be in a good position to recapture some of the growth in international activity that slipped away from its grasp during the 1980s; but the city may also be confronted by a renewed challenge from second tier financial centers—Los Angeles, Chicago, Toronto, and others throughout North America.

It is to a somewhat similar conclusion that Dennis Weatherstone arrives in "A U.S. Perspective on Europe 1992."

In his chapter, Weatherstone projects what the implications of Europe 1992—the European Community's deadline to remove its remaining barriers to a fully integrated internal market for goods and services—might be for both Europe itself and the United States. He ventures that the standardization of banking regulations and the lifting of controls on capital movement throughout the EC will likely benefit Paris, Frankfurt, Milan, or even New York, by weakening London's current competitive advantage. At the same time, he sees that the EC's demand for "reciprocity" will put new pressures on both Tokyo and New York to further liberalize access to their own markets.

The previous remarks are only sketches of chapters that have much greater bite to them than can be expressed in a few paragraphs. Also, this short overview is not meant to ignore possible differences of opinion among the six authors. In the end, however, it is remarkable that all six authors agree that New York is entering a new phase in its development as an international financial center and that preparing for the future will require a much more proactive role on the part of state and local officials than was needed in the past.

Notes

1. Samuel Ehrenhalt, Regional Commissioner of the U.S. Department of Labor, during his March 1988 monthly press conference.

2. "U.S. Court Backs Fed Rule on Bank Power" and "EC Finance Ministers Agree to Liberalize Capital Flow," *Wall Street Journal*, June 14, 1988.

3. "Agreements on Banks' Capital Set: 12-Nation Accord Forces Institutions to Raise Billions," *New York Times*, July 12, 1988, p. D1.

2

International Stock Market Transactions

Roy C. Smith

Financial markets around the world have become linked as never before into a single global pool of funds that can be accessed by users of funds and investors from all of the industrialized countries. Market centers have formed around the main areas of financial activity—New York, London, and Tokyo. These centers act as the principal linkages between domestic market participants and the markets serviced by other centers. They also serve as continental "hubs" attracting business and activity from satellite financial subcenters such as Boston, Chicago, and Toronto in the case of New York; Paris and Frankfurt in the case of London; and Hong Kong, Osaka, and Singapore in the case of Tokyo. This chapter describes the current activities in international stock market transactions, both those that involve new issues of equity securities and those that occur in secondary markets. It also explores the expanding role of New York City as one of the global financial centers in the market for international equity transactions.

International Equity Transactions

Within the last few years international transactions in equity securities have expanded enormously, as reflected in the substantial increase in cross-border transactions in secondary markets and by new issues offered to investors under one of several different "globalized" distribution techniques. This market phenomenon is the result of the convergence of many factors which have led toward the integration of capital markets around the world, factors such as the opening up of national markets through various deregulatory processes, the substantial improvements in financial information gathering and dissemination technology, and the growing involvement of major financial institutions as investors and providers of services to the markets.

As rapidly as the volume in international equity transactions has grown, only modest progress has been realized in terms of the integration of the different stock markets of the world. Considerable differences continue to exist in the methods the markets use to value shares and in the area of commissions, trading practices, new issue regulation, and settlement procedures. For many of these differences, a long time will be required before (or if) common ground can be reached. In other cases, some movement toward an international standard is clearly in evidence. Precedents occurring in one market will be observed and emulated by others. The abolition of fixed commission rates by the New York Stock Exchange in May of 1975 ("Mayday") generated a number of changes in equity markets, not only in New York but in London, Toronto, Zurich, Tokyo, and Sydney as well. In less than a decade many of the principles established as a result of Mayday were adopted by these other markets.

In general terms there are three types of international equity transactions: (1) those in which investors and issuers (e.g., from the United States) tap equity market resources in other countries to enhance the market liquidity that is available domestically; (2) those in which international markets are used (e.g., by Europeans) because the domestic market cannot meet the requirements of domestic participants; and (3) those in which the international markets are employed (e.g., by Japanese) as a way to avoid domestic market restrictions and entanglements. As in the case of the Eurobond market, the lack of regulation and the presence of a large, highly diversified, and very liquid pool of international investment funds has caused equity markets to evolve and develop internationally in such a way as to provide something for everyone.

This process has begun but is a long way from being finished. Much of what is now happening in international equity markets was just invented and not all of it will survive future innovations. Almost everything that is happening, however, contributes to the laying in of a foundation for a future, more integrated, international market. For these reasons, this is a uniquely instructive time to observe how a new market operating in a free international environment is formed, or perhaps, how it forms itself.

The international equities market is not a clone of the Eurobond market (though on occasion it travels down the same path), but it has proven to be equally resourceful in adapting itself to the new and varied requirements of its principal users. As in the Eurobond market, this free market adaptation is watched by domestic regulators and as a result is likely to play back into national markets some of its more successful experiences. For example, discussions have been underway between the securities regulatory authorities of the United States, the United Kingdom, and Canada regarding common new issue prospectus requirements; undoubtedly future rounds will help to standardize new issue requirements for other countries, shareholder voting entitlements, and various trading regulations and procedures, including rules to prevent insider trading.

Evolution of the Market

Participation in international equity investments is comparatively new for U.S. and Japanese investors but not for Europeans. For many years the most international of all investors were the Swiss banks who managed money on behalf of their many overseas customers. There was very little to invest in in Switzerland so Swiss banks looked abroad for suitable investment opportunities. During the 1960s and 1970s Swiss banks were the principal foreign investors in U.S. stocks; subsequently they became substantial investors in Japanese stocks as well. Similar to the Swiss banks, which for many years had attracted foreign "safekeeping" deposits, were banks and investment companies in Holland, Belgium, and Luxembourg—countries in which few good investment opportunities existed.

Just behind the Swiss as international investors might have appeared the British who have had a long history of overseas portfolio investment. Until 1979, however, Britain was subject to foreign exchange controls requiring that a premium be paid for foreign currency invested outside the country. Most other European countries have had similar foreign exchange regulations, though most have now been abolished. Once foreign exchange controls were lifted in the United Kingdom, a substantial increase in overseas investment, mostly in the United States and Japan, took place. Institutional investors in the United Kingdom have greatly increased their activities abroad and now hold and trade substantial volumes of international securities of all types. In the last few years, U.S. and Japanese institutional investors have also entered into active programs for investing in international equities. As a result, the international pool of funds participating in equities has greatly increased.

U.S. investment managers were forced by competitive pressures to improve investment performance. To do this, it was important to diversify holdings into stocks in other markets where not only market performance would be counted but also foreign exchange gains or losses. As more and more foreign opportunities were presented to U.S. investors, they learned more about investing abroad and began in the early 1980s to do so extensively.

TABLE 2.1
Foreign Investment of Private Sector Pension Assets, 1980, 1985, 1990 (in $ millions)

	1980	1985	1990
United States	$3,300	$27,000	$129,300
Britain	9,700	34,400	84,200
Japan	400	7,600	47,200
Netherlands	1,500	5,400	15,900
Canada	2,000	4,100	9,000
Switzerland	1,300	1,700	6,900
Rest of World	n/a	1,500	6,400
W. Germany	500	1,000	3,500
Ireland	300	700	1,400
Australia	0	500	3,700
Belgium	275	500	1,100
France	75	200	600
Total	$19,350	$84,600	$309,400

Source: InterSec Research Corp., *Foreign Investment of Private Sector Pensions Funds 1980-1990*, 1988.

Japanese institutional investors until recently were subject to foreign exchange controls limiting their investment abroad. Accordingly, they had not learned much about foreign markets, nor were they familiar with particular stocks and how they were valued. After foreign portfolio investment was freed up Japanese investors mainly concentrated their activities in the bond markets, principally buying U.S. Treasuries.

By 1986, however, as foreign exchange losses began eating into Japanese investors' returns on bond investments, they shifted to the equity markets. They were attracted to foreign equities by the prospect of larger capital gains and because of their low valuation and high dividend yields compared to Japanese equities which had risen to exceptional price levels.

Among new participants in international equities markets over the past few years have been pension funds, many of which have continued to enjoy a substantial inflow of funds each year and thus find their overall investment funds growing rapidly. Not only have total pension assets grown; the percentage of total assets invested in foreign securities also has increased substantially. This has been true for pension funds in countries all over the world, as Table 2.1 illustrates.

Japanese pension funds have been growing very rapidly as the country adjusts to the changing demographics of an aging population which has had insufficient pension plans in the past. Pension assets in Japan have grown by more than 20 percent per year since 1980.[1] An increasing amount of this money, which is managed by insurance companies and trust banks, will be invested in international equities. Altogether, Japanese investors who purchased only about $1 billion of U.S. equities in 1980, were expected, prior to the market crash in October 1987, to acquire more than $22 billion in 1987. The crash not only slowed their purchases considerably but also resulted in substantial net sales during the fourth quarter of 1987, resulting in purchases for the full year of only $12 billion. Purchases resumed in early 1988, however.

U.S. pension funds have also become very active as international investors; their exposure to foreign shares increased from about $22.5 billion at the end of 1985 to about $41.5 billion by the end of 1987. These investments were made while U.S. private pension funds were net sellers of U.S. equities, having sold (net of purchases) more than $47 billion from 1985 to 1987.[2]

There has also been substantial involvement in U.S. and Japanese equity markets by corporations—in the United States through mergers and acquisitions and corporate repurchase of shares, and in Japan by increasing intercorporate investment in shares of customers, suppliers, and by special investment trusts which have contributed greatly to the upward price movements. It is likely that this has helped to attract further foreign investment.

Advances in information and communications technology have been essential to the growth in the international equities market. Market information of all types is now available internationally, through newspapers, screens, and contact with brokers. Securities can also be traded internationally with a high degree of reliance on a trouble-free delivery, which was not always the case. The computerization of the international marketplace has made possible a level of expansion that probably could not otherwise have occurred. With this has come a large increase in the number of trained professionals who provide the many services needed to sustain a growing market: investment research information, trading and positioning capabilities, hedging, operations, and settlement facilities.

During the period of this great expansion of the international equities market, investment conditions have been extremely favorable and stock markets in virtually all countries powered their way to all-time highs. These market rises, sustained for several years and touching many separate markets, led to an unusually high level of enthusiasm for equity investments, including those abroad, until it was sharply curtailed by the worldwide collapse in October 1987. Some markets, the Japanese in particular, have recovered their earlier losses, and international activity has again revived, though not yet to the level of September 1987. Still, with the market support infrastructure in place, the free access to world markets intact, and the inclination of investment managers to look abroad

FIGURE 2.1
The World Equity Market, A Declining U.S. Share, 1975, 1988

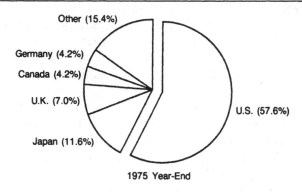

1975 Year-End

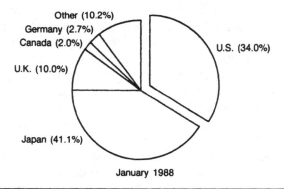

January 1988

Source: "FT—Actuaries World Indices," *Financial Times*, 1988.

for better performance opportunities still in force, it is unlikely that
even the fairly sharp price reversal that was experienced will deter the
growing participation in international equities for long. Indeed, many
investors realized several months after October 1987 that the performance
of funds that had remained invested in various international markets
was superior to that of funds which repatriated foreign investments at
the time of the crash, as many did.

Furthermore, one of the effects the bull markets and the exposure to
international opportunities has had upon U.S. money managers is a
recognition that the U.S. market is less than 35 percent of the world's
total market capitalization today and that a great many previously
unknown investment opportunities are available (see Figure 2.1).

At present, foreign equity investment is a two-way street for most countries. In the United States, net foreign portfolio investment in U.S. equities had increased to approximately $175 billion at the end of 1987, at a time when net U.S. investment in non-U.S. equities had increased to approximately $60 billion.[3] In the United Kingdom, both foreign investment in U.K. stocks and U.K. investments in foreign stocks are also rising. In Japan, high levels of foreign investment had been subject to some profit-taking during 1986 and 1987, but Japanese investment in overseas equities is rising rapidly. Throughout the world, institutional investors are adjusting their portfolios, sometimes for the first time, to achieve a comfortable portfolio mix between domestic and international equities. When the desired mix is achieved, notwithstanding year-to-year adjustments, the volume of international equity transactions may stabilize. This could be, but more likely a high level of trading in international portfolios (typical of performance-oriented institutional money management practices elsewhere) will result. If so, a large and permanent international trading environment would come into existence. This market, as is the Eurobond market to the world of debt instruments, could become equivalent in size and style of trading to the U.S. market.

Who the Investors Are

A brief look at the characteristics of the investors in the international equities market shows them to be substantially different in the United States, Europe, and Japan.

U.S. Investors

Institutional investors account for about 40 percent of share ownership in the United States but about 70 percent of share trading, over 50 percent in the form of large block trades. Accordingly, they are very active portfolio managers. The business of managing funds for others is extremely competitive and performance oriented in the United States, more so than anywhere else in the world. As a result, many investment managers have developed specialties—some have specialized in investing in foreign stocks, though as a group there are probably not more than 20 to 25 such managers who have been active overseas investors for more than the last ten years. In the last few years, however, most major investors have realized that higher net returns have been available in many overseas markets than were available in the United States and as a result have quickly turned themselves into international investors. (See Figure 2.2 for a comparison of five-year returns on stocks in five different markets.) Today approximately 200 U.S. institutional investors could be

FIGURE 2.2
World Equity Markets, 1982–1987

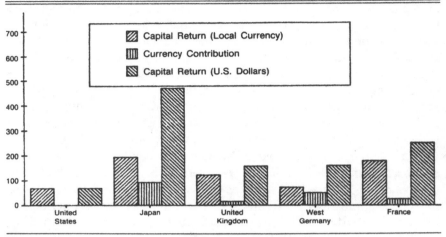

Source: "FT—Actuaries World Indices," *Financial Times*, 1988.

classified as active international equity investors. This number should increase as public funds and others as yet uncommitted to international investment become involved.

Many U.S. institutional investors have opened offices or set up subsidiaries abroad to manage their foreign investments more closely. These investors operate out of London, Geneva, Zurich, Tokyo, and other cities to combine local research coverage with good market sensitivity and execution. Other investors manage overseas investments from their U.S. offices, combining occasional visits abroad with research provided by U.S. and foreign brokers covering them at home. Still others have engaged overseas investment managers (frequently those from the United Kingdom) to manage a portion of their funds to be invested abroad. In covering U.S. investors in international equities, brokers must be somewhat ubiquitous, analysts as well as portfolio managers, covering the head office, the various field offices, and sometimes covering the United Kingdom or other foreign firm that is managing the U.S. investors' funds.

U.S. institutions have long encouraged competition and better service among brokers. They negotiate hard for lower commissions in markets where they can, or trade on a negotiated-rate basis off-the-market in cases where they cannot (e.g., Japan), thus adding to the pressure on the local exchanges to fully deregulate commission rates. They also seek brokers who will service their requirements for block and program trades and thus, somewhat unconsciously, serve as a role model for institutional investors in other countries who have started to trade more actively and aggressively as they themselves have become subject to higher standards of performance. Indeed, the heightened propensity to trade more actively and to force brokers to compete more aggressively for their business is clearly visible among U.K. institutional investors following London's "Big Bang." Big Bang has freed investors to act like U.S. institutional investors, and this is increasingly what they are doing.

The activity of U.S. investors in foreign markets has drawn many U.S. brokers into the business. The international research, trading, and sales specialists now employed by U.S. brokers serving the U.S. institutional investor community have grown significantly, both in number and in quality, over the past few years. The brokers do not, of course, confine their marketing of investment services for the U.K. market, for example, to U.S. investors; they also offer them to U.K. investors and those in other parts of the world. As the number of stocks covered in research and for which international trading markets are made increases, so does the penetration of the worldwide investor community by U.S. (and other) investment firms providing the best quality services. Gradually such competitive penetration will raise the standards of services available to all investors and this can be expected to further raise trading and competitive activity.

On balance, U.S. institutional participation has done more than add to the fund flows for international equities. It has also contributed significantly to the increasing trading activity in equity securities by major investors in other countries, by helping to bring more efficient U.S. practices to them.

European Investors

Figures are not available to tell us what percentage of the shares of European companies are owned by institutional investors, but one could guess that it would be a high percentage. Individual share ownership is comparatively small in most European countries where large banks, insurance companies, and investment trusts are the principal investors. These investors, however, have not been very active as traders, nor have they had especially active equity markets to trade in until very recently. Recent deregulation in Britain combined with many new issues of shares under government privatization programs has greatly increased trading in France. Market activity in general has also been increased in Switzerland, Germany, and Holland. European equity markets, until the October 1987 crash, had been lifted out of the doldrums of the past; the crash, however, has been a setback, though the markets are expected to resume trading at their more active pace in the future.

European equity investors, as in the case of investors in Eurobonds, can be divided into retail and institutional categories, with the retail group including mainly those individuals who invest through large continental banks. These banks, through their many branches, collect orders for brokerage transactions and for funds to be managed on a discretionary basis. Banks retain a large number of employed portfolio managers for this purpose. These will be supported by the bank's own research viewpoint and central guidance. Execution of orders is often done by each branch but can be centralized. Retail investors are especially sensitive to currency movements and to name recognition. Institutional investors, consisting of investment managers, insurance companies, pension funds, and banks, when investing in their own countries subscribe to local practices, but when investing internationally tend to behave similarly to U.S. institutional investors. These investors have shown a preference for U.S. and Japanese stocks over the years, though they have become active participants in the large new issues of European corporations that have come to the market over the past two years.

Japanese Investors

In Japan, approximately 69 percent of shares are owned by Japanese corporations or institutional investors and 6 percent by foreign institutional investors. Most of the shares owned by the Japanese corporations or institutions do not trade—they are held as part of long-term holdings that are based on intercorporate relationships. Approximately 42 percent of secondary market trading, however, is done by individuals who are, for the most part, exempt from capital gains taxes. This makes the Japanese market virtually the reverse of the U.S. market, in which most of the trading is done by institutions.

Except for the past two years, Japanese institutional and retail investors have not been active in foreign stock markets. This is because of the full range of high-performance investment opportunities in Japan, unfamiliarity with foreign shares, and until recently, regulatory restrictions. However, as the Japanese market rose to price levels reflecting a market-wide average price/earnings ratio of about 70, with negligible dividend yields, many investors began to look at the U.S. and European markets, which naturally appeared quite cheap to them. This casting abroad has been aided by the actions of aggressive Japanese securities firms that undertake to sell to retail investors throughout Japan large blocks of foreign shares accumulated through underwritings abroad.

Institutions in Japan which purchase foreign equities include investment companies (managed mainly by the principal Japanese securities companies), insurance companies, and Trust Banks, which manage corporate

TABLE 2.2
Foreign Investment in Japanese Securities and Japanese Investment in Foreign Securities,
1981–1987 (in $ millions)

Period	Long-Term Capital Outflow	Foreign Net Purchases of Japanese		Japanese Net Purchases of Non-Japanese		Current Account Surplus
		Equities	Bonds	Equities	Bonds	
1981	$ 9,672	$ 3,519	$ 5,772	$ 240	$ 5,808	$ 4,770
1982	14,969	1,613	4,861	151	6,076	6,850
1983	17,700	4,120	2,068	659	12,507	20,799
1984	49,651	(7,249)	3,456	50	26,773	35,003
1985	64,542	(3,111)	4,525	993	53,479	49,169
1986	131,461	(19,415)	(2,109)	7,048	93,024	85,845
1987						
Jan	12,461	(681)	227	113	10,460	4,841
Feb	11,441	(153)	(427)	1,523	9,411	7,634
Mar	8,307	(1,026)	334	2,903	3,331	8,487
Apr	12,393	(4,076)	1,149	1,988	7,485	8,152
May	12,778	(5,399)	(1,541)	1,894	5,446	7,112
Jun	19,194	(4,639)	(1,601)	1,598	12,336	7,498
Jul	18,515	(6,781)	(513)	1,462	8,938	7,284
Aug	1,134	(1,110)	3,311	491	6,175	5,396
Sept	2,374	(1,729)	3,398	1,559	1,983	8,509
Oct	18,476P	(13,094)	480	2,384	2,973	6,546P
Nov	14,133P	(8,835)	817	779	2,936	5,792P
Dec	5,921P	(977)	1,041	180	1,783	9,437P

Source: Japan Securities Research Institute, *Securities Markets in Japan, 1987* (Tokyo: 1987).

and individual pension funds. Apart from the investment companies, the most active institutions investing in foreign shares in recent years have been the Trust Banks, through special accounts called "Tokkin" (in which corporate funds are managed for investment on a favorable tax basis). These accounts reportedly have increased their investments in foreign equity securities severalfold since the beginning of 1987. Japanese investors, being latecomers to the international equities market, have only a negligible percentage of their funds in overseas equities. However, this has begun to change rapidly as investors have become more familiar with foreign markets. Japan's net investment in foreign equities and net investments in Japanese equities by foreigners are shown in Table 2.2.

Differences in Valuation

While it may be true that each national market values its equity securities in terms of similar views about how to determine what a future stream of dividends might be worth when capitalized at a locally suitable discount rate, it is also true that very great differences can exist between markets that are not explained by factors in the formula. In the United States, experienced financial institutions employing what they consider to be the most sophisticated tools for valuing securities tend to set prices. In Japan, fund managers with a large cash flow to invest and enthusiastic individual investors tend to follow the advice of stockbrokers who can create a kind of herd instinct that can move the market more than careful attention to market valuation formulae. In Europe, local markets may be so inactive in particular stocks that they appear undervalued by Americans looking for bargain investments which they believe in the long run will reflect "true" values. Many people feel they cannot apply their own valuation procedures to equities that are mainly traded in another country. Instead one must understand the market as locals do and go with the flow. Why else would a foreigner buy a Japanese bank stock at 40 times earnings hoping it would rise to 80 times earnings (which many Japanese bank stocks did in 1986–1987)?

On the other hand, as the markets become more closely linked (i.e., as foreign trading becomes as important as any other domestic source of trading), pricing mechanisms ought to converge. In many respects they have begun to do so.

Local investors, not being trading oriented, were not buying European shares. U.S. investors were, and offered prices to local institutions that they did not expect to get for large blocks. Europeans sold into a rising market created in part by foreigners who became a larger factor in valuing the shares. The "bargains" disappeared after a while, but so did some of the excessive concentration of local shareholdings. Local notions of valuations were altered by the foreign purchases. Another example could be the substantial amount of sales of Japanese equities by foreigners during 1986–1987—sales made in order to lock in high profits before the expected collapse of the overpriced Japanese market. Surely the selling pressure sent a message to the market, but this time the buyers included, in addition to Japanese individuals, Japanese corporations that were investing excess cash through Tokkin accounts in stocks with very large amounts of hidden assets. Banks, for example, were probably trading less on the value of their earnings than on the basis of "adjusted" book value, in which holdings of shares in hundreds of Japanese "clients" and priceless real estate assets would be marked to the market. Different markets sometimes appear to value similar equities in very different ways; but not surprisingly, when fuller knowledge is obtained of a specific situation, sometimes the unexplainable anomalies disappear.

FIGURE 2.3
Foreign Investors' Influence on Major Stock Markets

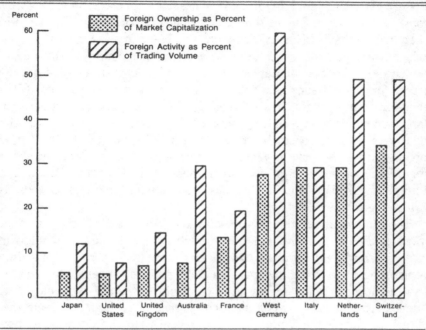

Source: Helen Troughton, *Japanese Finance. The Impact of Deregulation* (London: Euromoney Publications).

Figure 2.3 shows the differing percentages of foreign ownership and trading volume for different international equity markets. It would seem that those with high foreign involvement ought to have fewer price anomalies than those with low foreign involvement. With more experience in these markets more data can be obtained that might explain differences in valuation between markets somewhat better.

New Issues

Through the end of 1987, the U.S. domestic market continued to be the world's largest market for new issues of equity securities. Over 1,000 issues of common stocks and convertible debentures, aggregating approximately $54 billion, were offered in the United States during 1987. (In 1986, over 1,200 equity issues aggregating more than $60 billion were sold in the United States.) The 1987 totals include 40 non-U.S. equity issues with a market value of $5.1 billion (including $2.5 billion representing the U.S. tranche of the $12 billion British Petroleum sale by the British Government).[4]

International issues of two types tend to be offered in the United States: (1) issues sold by foreign companies to establish or improve markets for their shares in the United States or to obtain a higher price than would have been available in the home market and (2) issues which were part of larger offering schemes originating in Europe, in which the U.S. piece, or tranche, is marketed as part of a global offering (some of these issues are sold on a "private placement" basis and therefore not registered with the SEC). The U.S. market is attractive to large corporations and selling shareholders seeking broader distribution of their shares. Accordingly, most of the foreign volume in the United States during the past few years is accounted for by issues of shares (or ADRs) of such large companies as British Telecom, British Gas, Philips NV, British Airways, Barclays Bank, Telefonica, and most recently, British Petroleum.

The United States requires registration with the SEC of new issues to be offered to the public. Many foreign companies are very reluctant to go through this process which is extremely expensive and time-consuming for a company that has not previously been registered. As long as approximately the same pricing and terms are available in the home or Euro-equity market such companies often prefer to issue their securities outside the United States. In recent years, however, many non-U.S. companies have made efforts to educate investors in the United States about their shares, with the understanding that in due course the company would become a "reporting company" which files annual reports to the SEC in a form similar to what is required for a public offering registration statement. Despite the aversion to registration with the SEC, the benefits of having shares trade actively in the United States appears to be drawing a number of them toward becoming reporting companies.

Compared to the predominantly domestic U.S. new issues market, new issue activity in international equity securities was quite different. In 1986, its peak year, 394 issues of common stock, convertible debentures, or debt issues with equity purchase warrants were offered for a total value of approximately $32 billion, an amount nearly five times the international new issue volume of 1983. Of these issues, 61 (accounting for $6.5 billion) were Euro-equity issues of shares of European companies offered through a Euromarket syndicate. Two of these issues (Fiat, Daimler Benz) each exceeded $1 billion. In addition, the international market saw 77 new issues of convertible debentures totalling $6.5 billion. Most extraordinary, however, was the more than 100 issues of debt with equity purchase warrants aggregating over $15 billion by Japanese companies.[5] These issues which were offered as packages with extremely low coupon rates (as low as 1 percent), were stripped by investors into the warrants which were sold directly into Japan, and deep discount bonds which were bundled together and offered to other investors with an interest rate swap into floating rate notes. The bonds, on a floating rate LIBOR basis, would offer an attractive yield to Japanese banks and other investors.

The Japanese, as has become their practice in recent years, continue to use the Euromarket in substitution for their own more regulated and restrictive market, even though the investors in the securities they issue are for the most part other Japanese.

Distribution Methods

The practice is developing for large issues, in which a particular distribution of shares is desired, to organize simultaneous, coordinated distributions of shares in several national markets. The large British privatizations utilized this practice which was originally developed in 1984 for the issue of $1 billion of Texaco Euro-convertible debentures.

In the first British privatization distributed internationally, British Telecom in 1984, U.S., Canadian, European, and Japanese tranches were employed. For the subsequent, and much larger issue of British Gas in 1986 similar tranches were employed. Subsequent to the British Telecom issue, the practice of using separate foreign tranches spread to U.S. issuers; this method of distributing shares was quite widely accepted by U.S. companies seeking a more visible participation by non-U.S. investors and, in 1986, 32 such issues through combined U.S. and European syndicates occurred.

During 1987, 20.75 million shares of Philips NV (valued at approximately $500 million) were placed around the world through simultaneous offerings in the United States, the Netherlands, the United Kingdom, Switzerland, West Germany, Japan, and the "rest of the world." The largest tranche, accounting for 5.75 million shares, was sold in the United States through a registered public offering. Later in the year, a combined offering of 42.5 million shares of Barclays Bank plc (valued at $393 million) was offered simultaneously through separate issues in the United States and Japan.

The largest such international distribution was the sale of 2.2 billion shares of the British Petroleum Company (BP) in October 1987. The transaction, which was underwritten under the British method (see below) on October 15th, for subscription prior to October 28th, was divided about equally between the domestic U.K. market and the markets outside of the United Kingdom. The October 19th crash occurred during the subscription period, causing the offering to be almost completely unsubscribed. The underwriters were left with the entire issue. Four U.S. underwriters had committed between them to underwrite $1 billion of the BP shares in partly paid form to be sold in the United States. Among them the U.S. underwriters lost more than $250 million after taxes. In time the issue was distributed, and the market for BP shares returned to normal. The issue had been a disaster, but the international syndicate held, and did its job, despite extreme duress.

Multiple tranche issues have produced some conflicting views between U.S. firms and European (mainly continental) banks. The U.S. firms prefer a single syndicate, perhaps largely populated with international underwriters, to which shares are allocated in accordance with hard demand for the shares indicated by each syndicate member. On the assumption that the best sales effort is the most competitive one, no geographical restrictions would be observed (other than those required by law). Thus if Merrill Lynch's office in Frankfurt received large orders for the shares, which Merrill Lynch would report to the syndicate manager, then Merrill Lynch would be allocated shares accordingly. If Dresdner Bank had only modest demand from its portfolio managers, then Dresdner Bank might not be allocated any shares. The German market should be covered by those doing business in Germany, German or not. Furthermore, tight control of share allocations tends to ensure that shares get into the hands of investors who want them on the first try, so that shares do not have to be redistributed in the secondary markets in order to get to their highest priced investor. U.S. firms use this method of distribution within the United States to ensure tightly priced deals.

According to this view of the syndicate function, dual or multiple tranches are not necessary, indeed they may only serve to loosen up distribution within the separate tranches. Most U.S. syndicate managers, however, when organizing dual U.S./Euro-syndicates for U.S. issuers (which current practice—until the crash—required them to accommodate even if they were not convinced of all of the merits of the dual syndicate approach), will insist on a single "book-running" manager for both tranches. They will, in essence, treat the smaller European syndicate as if it were a part of the U.S. syndicate, and allocate shares to its members strictly in accordance with demand. Otherwise the danger exists that European syndicate members who have only weak demand from cus-tomers may try to sell the shares into the grey market in Europe or to another dealer who probably would sell them back into the U.S. market where a fixed price offering is underway. This actually occurred in some of the early dual syndicate issues in 1985. Many syndicate managers believe that the dual syndicate adds very little to the distribution, and when required to oblige clients who want them, makes the European members fight hard to get shares allocated to them.

The European view is quite different. They like separate tranches because it is a way of enforcing market discipline, provides a lot of focus and attention to the issue within each tranche, and relies on what European banks do best, which is to underwrite shares which their clients are invited to subscribe to, with the bank being prepared to "sit on" any unsold portion for an indefinite time. Large corporate issues and privatizations can work very successfully through such a system (e.g., Daimler Benz, the British and French privatization issues, etc.). However, if the issue is not fully subscribed, or is uninspired, then a great run to dump shares into the home market can occur which can have extremely severe consequences for the issue. The large sale ($2.36 billion) of Fiat during 1986 was an example of how multiple tranche, European-style issues can go wrong.

It can be expected that underwriters from each different area that might be represented by a tranche will argue that a tranche in his particular area makes great sense, even if other tranches do not.

In order to secure high participation by investors in any tranche area it is usually necessary to structure the distribution in that area as a public offering, which requires registration of offering documents with national authorities. The United States and Japan have the strictest rules governing the registration of securities, though both markets can be approached on "private placement" bases in which sales efforts are restricted to qualified (i.e., sophisticated, usually institutional) investors. U.S. firms have argued that the most practical, yet fully global distribution is achieved through an offering that is registered with the SEC, with a syndicate led by a U.S. firm that includes major international banks and securities firms from around the world with vigorous marketing efforts to be conducted in Europe and Japan, as well as the United States, but share allocation to be determined on the basis of solid demand. It is perhaps not surprising that European and Japanese firms have their own version of the optimal global distribution method.

Underwriting

U.S. underwriting procedures are designed to obtain the highest price for the seller of securities. This is done by forming a syndicate of securities firms that will agree to purchase the shares from the seller, and resell them immediately to investors. The price is not fixed until just before the offering is made to the public, after a period during which salesmen from the underwriters have marketed the issue to their customers and developed a "feel" for the price level needed to sell the shares without a big price run-up in the after-market. A successful issue is one in which the entire issue moves into investors' hands at the offering price and the issue opens at a premium of no more than about 10 percent. The underwriting syndicate in such an issue is only exposed to a minimal holding period between the purchase and the confirmation of sales with customers. Of course, if the issue is mispriced or the market changes before the distribution is complete, underwriters can suffer losses. They are compensated for this risk, however, and most underwriters are comfortable with it.

The Euromarket uses U.S. underwriting procedures for the most part. Important differences exist in the lack of a fixed offering price to investors and in certain legal aspects but the principles and objectives are similar. International equity markets can be volatile and underwriters have suffered losses on a number of issues.

In the United Kingdom, and in many other parts of Europe, an older system of underwriting is used, which many people refer to as the "British" underwriting method. In this system, the announcement of the transaction and the offering price occur at the same time. A syndicate of underwriters is formed to "backstop" the issue, which is then made available to investors on a subscription basis during a two-to-three-week subscription period (during the whole of which the underwriters are at risk). At the expiration of the subscription period, the applications for shares are counted up; any shortfall is purchased by the underwriters who for the most part are insurance companies and other institutional investors. Apart from arranging the underwriting syndicate, brokers have little to do in the process. Nor do the underwriters, including the lead merchant bank handling the issue, have much to do with marketing. This system recognizes that the main institutional investors in the market will be the likely buyers; as an incentive to get them in they are paid an underwriting fee for using their capital to prop up the issue while individual and other investors go through the subscription process. The definition of a successful issue is one that is fully subscribed; in fact, some believe the more oversubscribed, the more successful. Unfortunately, such oversubscription tends to result in a sharp rise in the stock price when it is free to trade (or put another way, the subscription price tends to be set sufficiently low to be sure that oversubscription occurs). On the other hand, if the issue is undersubscribed, the underwriters can sustain substantial losses, as the British Petroleum issue more than amply demonstrated.

The British method is still in use in the United Kingdom, although the recent success of several very large privatization issues has resulted in some modest tinkering with the program—mainly by circulating a preliminary prospectus (a "pathfinder" in their terms) without a price to feel out the market first. It is probable that following the many changes in the U.K. market resulting from Big Bang, and the failure of the British Petroleum and several other underwritings during 1987, that the British underwriting method will be further changed in the future.

Secondary Trading

Secondary trading in international stocks has been conducted in most financial centers for many years. Sometimes the shares have been listed on principal exchanges; often they have not been, instead being the object of small over-the-counter activity by firms specializing in international stocks. For years the principal activity was foreign stock arbitrage, in which one would buy an ADR of, say, a Dutch stock and simultaneously sell the number of underlying shares represented by the ADR in Amsterdam. To do this profitably one must be a master of the details involved; the purchase in dollars after commissions must cost less than the proceeds of the sale of the shares, after commissions and transfer expenses, and after the foreign exchange costs of converting back into dollars. Such arbitrage activities have kept prices of international shares around the world in line with their home market values.

The next development was to provide market-making services to customers interested in buying foreign securities that were not available on exchanges. For example, a U.S. pension fund might want to buy shares in Fujitsu Ltd. which is not listed on any U.S. exchange or in NASDAQ, but for which ADRs are available. The pension fund might call a Japanese broker based in New York who could say, "We will take your order and purchase Fujitsu shares overnight. We will confirm tomorrow and tell you at what dollar price the order was executed. We will then deposit the shares with the agent bank in Japan and have ADRs put into your account." Alternatively the pension fund might call a U.S. market-maker in Fujitsu and be told, "We will sell you Fujitsu dollar ADRs right now for $x." The U.S. broker, if he does not have Fujitsu ADRs in inventory will try to buy them in the New York market or trade with a Japanese broker overnight to get the shares to deliver to the pension fund. The market-maker's price will reflect the various uncertainties he must contend with. Over time, the volume in international equities has built up considerably and pricing has been tightened up accordingly.

In the last few years several further developments have improved secondary trading in international stocks. First, U.S. and other firms have begun making over-the-counter markets in listed U.S. shares in London in the morning before the New York Exchange opened. This has improved liquidity in U.S. shares for European investors to some extent.

Second, with foreign membership now available on London and Tokyo, as well as New York, stock exchanges, it is now possible for participating firms to be active market-makers in U.S., British, and Japanese stocks around the clock. Such firms are able to balance orders from all over the world, not just from their home market.

Third, institutional investors are increasingly placing portions of the funds under their management into international stocks. Many such investments are done actively and require selection from among many different stocks in the same industry. Such choices require research and information from many sources. Other investments are passive, that is they are made according to a system for indexing. Several indexes now exist, as does the capability for program and large block trading in non-U.S. equities.

Fourth, the commitment to dealing in international equities by major firms is very substantial and is reflected in the number of personnel that have been added in research, trading, sales coverage, systems and back office, and foreign exchange by major U.S., British, Japanese, and other firms. A very large increase in market infrastructure has occurred which not only makes improved services possible but also provides competitive energy in the market as all of these new employees seek to advance their careers.

Fifth, the improvement in market information in international shares is also very important. More foreign stocks are now traded on the New York Stock Exchange and in the highly efficient NASDAQ System. In London, many foreign shares are listed in London and now traded in the new London market, a system similar to NASDAQ. In Tokyo, many foreign shares are listed on the Tokyo Stock Exchange with quite a few others in preparation. It is possible now to receive a reliable quote on virtually any stock, whose home market is one of the major financial centers, from just about anywhere on the telephone. Quotes are also available for securities from many other countries on very short notice.

Finally, there are the changes created by Big Bang, the reconstitution of the London Stock Exchange. These may be the most significant and far-reaching changes that have occurred, thus far, in international equity markets. Since October 1986, London has given up all of its long-standing securities market practices and has adopted, in their place, procedures that are almost identical to those in use in the United States. Not only will these steps make the London market more efficient, they will make it much more compatible with the U.S. market. Big Bang stands as a monumental example to other Europeans who will in time (supposedly by 1992) need to conform their national securities markets to international standards and practices. It will not be long before the U.S. and British electronic markets are merged (in terms of trading activity). With this may also come a further merging of market practices, regulation, and infrastructure, leading to a dominant English-speaking financial marketplace that others will wish to join. As it spreads, so will the prospects for equity market integration around the world.

Issues and Trends for the Future

A lot has happened in a very short time to the international equities market, and much is happening yet. International activity in equity markets gives every indication of being a permanent and growing feature of the investment business. As international ownership increases there is reason to think that valuation will converge toward a loose sort of international standard.

New methods of international distribution are being tried. In time, perhaps a common practice will evolve; if so, it will have to be one that makes suitable room for all those market participants capable and desirous of a role. The greatest competitive energy, however, appears to be behind the traditional U.S. notion of hard-working brokers developing clients who respond to service and put in orders, as opposed to portfolio managers who wait for clients to ask for advice or to have something done.

The demand for services to professional investors will rise to U.S. levels in newly liberated Britain and institutions on the continent will watch closely to see how things work out. As U.S. practices become the norm in London, British institutions will (as indeed they have already done) become much more active traders, and their portfolios will become more aggressively and better managed. New standards of investment performance will be adopted, which will create more competition, more services, and result in better, more liquid markets for British and perhaps all other European equities which may find the bulk of their trading activity gravitating to London. British companies, and in time, other European companies, will become more active issuers of equity securities of various types. And so on, ultimately to find Japan included in the embrace.

Until Big Bang, equity markets outside the United States had been locked into an old-fashioned, highly national environment that lacked competition and opportunity. Prior to Mayday (1975) our markets in the United States were similarly constrained. Since Big Bang, there have been important liberalizations in other equity markets, notably Canada, Australia, and Japan. It appears inevitable that much further change lies ahead; in many ways the process of conversion from national to international markets has just begun.

The Role of New York City

Of the three major international finance centers, New York has the brightest future. For many reasons, including the following, analysts can expect the role and importance of New York City as an international financial capital to grow significantly:

1. Despite the crash of October 1987, the volume of international equity transactions is expected to grow steadily over the coming years as U.S. institutional investors increase their investments abroad, and as more Japanese and European investors increase their holdings in the United States. Most of these transactions will pass through brokers located in New York City.

2. Relative to London and the Eurobond market, the United States is a relative latecomer to international finance. Many U.S. companies still have no significant foreign stockholders, and many U.S. institutional investors, especially public sector pension funds, have not yet made significant international equity investments. Compared to their European counterparts, the internationalization of U.S. finance has a long way to go. As it does, the volume of secondary market activity in international stocks carried out in New York City will be increased accordingly, and at a faster rate than in Europe.

3. This growth in trading and related activity will attract more professionals to New York. Some will be added to the staff of U.S. firms, others will be employed by European and Asian banks and brokers. More companies will want their shares traded on markets in New York. More visitors will come to New York to consult with international equity market professionals located here.

4. U.S. and other firms will recognize that New York City is by far the lowest cost location in which to conduct high-quality international financial service activities. Especially with the adjustment in the foreign exchange value of the dollar, wage, telecommunications, and occupancy costs are far lower than in Tokyo or in London. U.S. firms are reducing staff in London, and repatriating U.S. nationals to New York when they can. All participants in the international financial markets know that overseas business is more expensive to conduct than domestic, and that it is vital if a firm is to succeed in international business to reduce the overseas overhead associated with it, partly by carrying out many of the operations and related functions for overseas transactions in the head office of the firm, and partly by increasing employment of local

personnel abroad. Compared to the other principal cities, New York offers a significant cost advantage.

Despite such factors, officials of New York State and New York.City must remember that the international financial community is mobile. If the cost advantages disappear, London may look attractive again, or Toronto. There will always be alternatives to New York, which adverse changes in taxation or in regulation could cause those in the international business to inspect carefully.

Notes

1. InterSec Research Corp., *Foreign Investment of Private Sector Pension Funds 1980–1990*, 1988.

2. InterSec Research Corp., *Foreign Investment* and Steven Einhorn and Patricia Sangkuan, "Equities—Supply and Demand," *Portfolio Strategy*, Goldman Sachs & Co., March 1988.

3. InterSec Research Corp., *Foreign Investment*; Einhorn and Sangkuan, "Equities—Supply and Demand"; Michael Sesit, "Japanese Investors Wrest From British No. 1 Rank as Net Foreign Buyers," *The Wall Street Journal*, April 8, 1988.

4. IDD Information Service.

5. IDD Information Service and Einhorn and Sangkuan, "Equities—Supply and Demand."

Bibliography

Bush, Janet, et al. "A Glum 100 Days," *Financial Times* (London). January 27, 1988.

Elliot, Charles, and Akers, Nicholas. *Japan Investment Strategy Highlights*. February/March 1988. New York: Goldman Sachs & Co., 1988.

Jones, Rosamund. "Annual Global Equity Report," *Euromoney*. May, 1987.

Kamijo, Toshiaki. "Securities Markets and Investment Banking in Japan." *Investment Banking Handbook*, ed. J. Peter Williamson. New York: John Wiley and Son, Inc., 1988.

Schwartz, Robert A. *Equity Markets*. New York: Harper and Row, 1988.

Spicer and Oppenheim, eds. *International Equities*. London: IFR Publishing Ltd., 1986.

3

The Foreign Challenge to U.S. Commercial Banks

Robert B. Cohen

Is there a competitive threat to U.S. commercial banks? If so, what can be done about it? For Americans, who have been shocked by the fall from primacy of the U.S. auto, steel, and semiconductor industries, the threat from Japanese and European banks is becoming a serious concern. But how real is the threat? Don't U.S. banks still have a sophistication that cannot be matched by their competitors? Is there any parallel between the way Honda and Datsun once shipped low-cost compact cars to the U.S. market and the way Japanese banks have rapidly obtained market share by competing for the commodity-like part of banking business—the commercial and industrial loans, treasury bonds, etc.—where profit rates are especially low?[1]

These questions are difficult to answer because a technique to evaluate the competitive strength of banks has yet to be developed. Thus far, little competitive analysis has been done in any of the services.[2] What is needed is a means to evaluate the competitive strength of individual banks or groups of banks from one nation. A general approach can be derived from studies of industrial competitiveness, however, since measures of bank performance parallel the yardsticks used in industrial sectors. These measures include: size, international market scope and involvement, cost of capital, productivity, profitability, innovativeness, and product sophistication.

This chapter examines some of the competitive advantages of U.S. and foreign banks and draws a number of guarded conclusions about the seriousness of the foreign challenge to U.S. commercial banks. The competitive advantages of the largest global foreign banks are usually cited as large asset bases, close ties to clients, highly profitable operations,

TABLE 3.1
Market Value of Major International Banks, 1987 (in $ billions)

Rank	Name	Market Capitalization
1	Sumitomo	$58.9
10	Tokai	27.4
32	J.P. Morgan	6.5
100	Banco Popular-Spain	1.9
—	Chase	1.8

Source: "Global Finance Rankings," *Wall Street Journal*, September 18, 1987, p. 31D.

ability to focus on the long run, and advantages gained from favorable national banking laws. The national laws have permitted universal banking in Germany, Switzerland, and the United Kingdom and low returns on assets in Japan and France that enabled banks to buy a large market share.

By contrast, major U.S. banks are usually considered to be very innovative, characterized by high levels of productivity, well established in profitable, high value-added banking services, and, in a number of cases, extensively invested in global communications and service networks. This chapter reviews a number of indicators of competitive strength in order to ascertain what are the advantages of each group of banks. The first part examines the new setting for banking, pointing to the rapid expansion of Japanese banks in international markets and considering the impact of new capital adequacy standards and of dramatic changes in the structure of markets. It is followed by a lengthy section evaluating the competitive strengths of U.S. banks. The chapter concludes with a number of points derived from the information discussed during the evaluation of competitive strength.

The New Setting for Banking

Most evidence points to the fact that U.S. commercial banks are being challenged at home and abroad as never before. International rankings indicate that Japanese *banks* have become the largest in the world. Indeed, several have market values in the $60 billion range (Sumitomo, Industrial Bank of Japan), ten times larger than that of the largest U.S. banks, such as J.P. Morgan (Table 3.1).

In the Euromarkets, Japanese banks have challenged the traditional leaders in syndications of new international bond underwriting and international loan business. Last year, Japanese banks occupied many of the top ranks in the "league" tables for managing Eurobond issues. In the United States, foreign banks accounted for 16 percent of all commercial and industrial loans in 1987, with the Japanese accounting for nearly 9 percent of these loans (Figure 3.1). Abroad, as Robert Heller of the Federal Reserve Board recently noted, U.S. banks are pulling back from their commitment to international banking, except in rapidly growing centers such as London and Tokyo.[3] Japanese banks now have the largest overseas network of branches and agencies, 676 in 1985 compared to just 30 in 1961.[4] While other challengers, such as the British, have also pulled back from the substantial international exposure they had in the 1960s, the largest Japanese global banks have established a strong global presence that should translate into competitive advantage in the future.

Competition between U.S. and foreign banks needs to be evaluated by looking at both the "firepower," or asset strength, of the largest banks, and other factors that can shape the business environment. Changes in capital adequacy standards are likely to shift competitiveness, as may modifications to the Glass-Steagall Act in the United States. But as in the auto or steel industries, productivity, cost of capital, relative profitability, and other factors are also important, especially the evolution of these factors over time. Since measures of banking competitiveness are not well defined, close approximations may need to be employed at first, such as using operating expenses and net income per employee to measure productivity or using the ratio of market value to capitalization to provide some measure of the costs of raising new funds.

The capital adequacy standards being negotiated under the auspices of the Bank for International Settlements (BIS) will raise capital requirements substantially. Most analysts view the adjustment to these new standards as more of a problem for U.S. banks than for their Japanese, Swiss, and West German competitors.[5] However, if Japanese banks are allowed to use only 40 percent of their hidden reserves to meet the new requirements for secondary capital, these standards could become a significant problem for the leading Japanese international and city banks.[6]

The new capital adequacy standards may permit foreign banks that possess substantial liquidity to gain competitive advantages. Quite a few of the world's current largest banks, particularly those from the United States, would be constrained by a lack of adequate funds. As a result, they would have much greater difficulty entering new markets and developing new products. In the short run, this might enable a small group of international banks to gain some competitive advantage by establishing an oligopolistic market for certain bank products and services. For example, were these banks able to raise profit margins on

FIGURE 3.1
Foreign C&I Loans as a Percentage of Total C&I Loans in the United States, 1973–1987

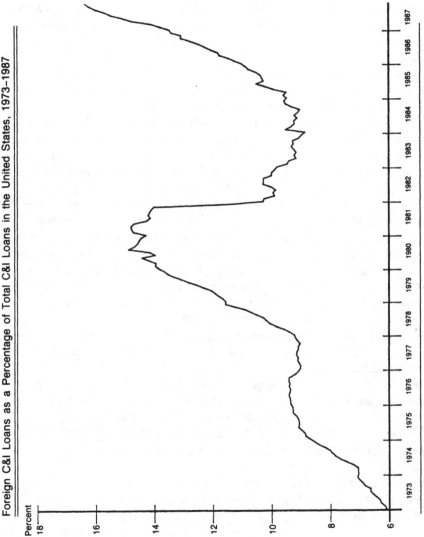

Note: Commercial and Industrial (C&I) loans by U.S. branches of foreign banks as a percentage of C&I loans by all domestic and foreign commercial banking institutions in the United States.

Source: Federal Reserve Board, 1988.

government and corporate loans to levels more lucrative than those of the 1980s, their profitability and their ability to increase their capital base would be dramatically altered.

Although the new capital adequacy standards may exert a significant influence on the development of the U.S. banking sector over the next five to ten years, a number of bankers would argue that their ability to build a strong, innovative base of services and/or a strong retail network could be far more important in determining competitive strength. Such bankers are buttressed in their thinking by at least one study that argues that the growth of large Japanese banks has been driven by the appreciation of the yen and the growth of the Japanese surplus, rather than any strength inherent in the Japanese banks.[7]

In addition, the dynamic of change in banking markets argues that structural changes will be the key determinants of competitiveness. First, markets are changing dramatically, with the main financial products—corporate loans—becoming high-volume, low-profit margin items and with much of the profits earned by banks coming from other services, including some services not directly counted on their balance sheets—foreign exchange trading, standby letters of credit, etc. Success in exploiting the profitability of these services could give U.S. money center banks advantages that many analysts now believe are accessible only to large U.S. regional banks, particularly if the money center banks can reduce their exposure to LDC loans.

Second, the rise of regional banks may transform the U.S. banking industry profoundly. Were regional banks to continue to grow in size and to raise new funds for expansion relatively easily, they might soon become the true rivals of the large foreign banks that now see Citicorp, Chase, Morgan, and Manufacturers Hanover as their competition. Indeed, the recent crash has made many regionals stronger and would support this line of reasoning.[8] While such a shift would mark a watershed in U.S. banking, it appears more likely to occur, subsequent to the events of October 19, 1987. In addition, passage of the Proxmire Bill in the Congress should modify Glass-Steagall regulations enough to give new power to the regionals. Still, there could be other structural changes in the industry, such as those suggested by the recent discussions between Credit Suisse and First Boston, namely, mergers of commercial and investment banks, including cross-border mergers.

Finally, U.S. money center banks have been adjusting their strategies to be more like the Japanese. They are altering their decisionmaking capacity so that they can take advantage of opportunities that offer substantial profits. For instance, Citicorp controls dollar-peso exchanges in the Philippines and another large U.S. bank has a significant position in dollar-yen clearing for Japanese banks.

While the discussion, thus far, has focused principally on the rising challenge from Japanese banks, a number of large European banks are also playing an important role in shaping the global competitive picture in banking. These banks must be considered in any rigorous competitive analysis. They include the major banks from West Germany, Switzerland, France, and Britain. With the possible exception of the British banks, they too have been placing great emphasis on establishing a global presence.

Evaluating the Competitive Strengths
of U.S. Banks

Competition in financial services is based on several dimensions: first, the asset size of institutions, which gives them the scale and scope of products and geographical coverage often required by large clients or those operating in more complex markets; second, the cost of capital, since firms with cheaper capital can offer more competitive rates than those that must pay more for their funds; third, the ability to establish close relationships with important clients, although the importance of this factor has eroded in the United States and to a lesser degree in Europe; fourth, the ability to put together deals, where skills, organization, and expertise carry a real premium; fifth, the ability to create linkages between financial institutions that offer some advantages in obtaining funds and servicing clients; and sixth, the creation of a global financial network that can provide a means to source funds and to service clients. This section reviews a number of these dimensions of competitiveness.

Firepower

As noted in Table 3.1, Sumitomo, the largest Japanese bank, was nearly ten times the size of J.P. Morgan and nearly 30 times as large as Chase in terms of market value at the end of 1987. This reflects the fact that Japanese banks have grown quite large as the Japanese economy has expanded and have grown disproportionately in dollar terms as the dollar exchange rate has fallen, as noted in Table 3.2. What power does large size provide for banks? If foreign banks can translate size into a large and effective funding and service network and into an organization skilled in evaluating credit and exchange rate risk, then size can permit foreign banks and securities firms to develop the innovative ideas and

TABLE 3.2
Assets of World's 100 Largest Banks, 1969, 1986

	1986	1969
U.S. Banks	12.0%	33.5%
Japanese Banks	39.7%	17.1%

Source: *The Banker* as cited in Thomas H. Hanley et al., "Domestic and International Bank Stock Investing: A Global Approach," Salomon Brothers Inc. Research Department, March 1988, p. 6.

deal-making expertise that are often required to become more competitive. Of course, size itself does not guarantee that these skills will be developed.

Size, coupled with a strong credit rating, can be especially important in developing strong relationships with the largest corporations. It is the U.S. *Fortune* 1000 firms that have received the greatest attention from foreign banks and securities firms. The fact that many foreign banks have maintained a Triple A credit rating (see Table 3.3) while J.P. Morgan alone among the U.S. banks has retained such credit-standing, gives the foreigners distinct advantages in attracting corporate deposits, assembling loan syndicates, or underwriting Eurodollar issues. A higher rating means that the foreign banks can borrow funds more cheaply than others and offer corporations loans at lower spreads over the basic rate than their U.S. competitors. Given the large amount of funds required by multinational corporations around the globe, the inability to supply large quantities of funds at a competitive price, in turn, means that U.S. banks do not have access to the amounts of capital needed to enable them to compete internationally.

However, if one looks at this ability to provide funds from a very broad perspective, by using not only the assets owned by a financial institution but also those that it manages as a measure of "placing power," a very different ranking appears (see Table 3.4). While the Japanese and Swiss banks are still among those with substantial "placing power," Prudential, American Express, Citicorp, and Metropolitan Life are in the top 10. If there are close ties among U.S. institutions, especially among insurance companies, banks, and securities firms, U.S. lenders are likely to have more true firepower, in the eyes of corporate borrowers, than is suggested by more traditional measures of bank power, such as market capitalization and asset rankings.

Among the largest Continental European banks, capital strength, superior profitability, and perceived greater integrity of their loan portfolio has led to a belief that they will remain formidable competitors on a global scale. In addition, these banks are universal in nature, competing

TABLE 3.3
Top-Rated Banks and Securities Firms, Long-Term Credit Rating, February 1987

	Moody's	S & P
Morgan	Aaa	AAA
Barclays	Aaa	AA+
Nat West	Aaa	AA+
BNP	Aaa	AA+
Societe Generale	Aaa	AA+
Credit Lyonnais	Aaa	—
UBS	Aaa	AAA
Credit Suisse	Aaa	AAA
Swiss Bank Corp.	Aaa	AAA
Deutche	Aaa	AAA
Dai-Ichi Kangyo	Aaa	—
Sumitomo Bank	Aaa	AA+
Mitsubishi Bank	Aaa	—
Ind. Bank of Japan	Aaa	AAA
Long-Term Credit Bank	Aaa	AA
Nomura Securities	—	AAA

Source: Ingo Walter, *Global Competition in Financial Services* (Cambridge, Mass.: Ballinger, 1988), Chapter 4.

TABLE 3.4
"Placing Power," Owned and Managed Assets, December 31, 1986 (in $ billions)

Rank	Financial Institution	Owned Assets	Managed Assets	Total[1]
1	Prudential	$104.5	$145.1	$249.6
2	Dai-Ichi Kangyo	215.4	28.7	244.1
3	Union Bank of Switzerland	93.6	150.0	243.6
4	American Express	99.5	140.0	239.5
5	Sumitomo Bank	184.7	51.5	236.2
6	Mitsubishi Bank	180.8	46.7	227.5
7	Citicorp	196.1	24.5	220.6
8	Swiss Bank Corp	84.8	130.0	214.8
9	Metropolitan Life	81.6	103.2	184.8
10	Credit Suisse	63.8	120.0	183.8

[1]Includes amounts of owned assets by parent firm that are double counted in managed assets. Adjustment for such double counting could not be made for most institutions. Adjusting for double counting changes Prudential's total to $153.7 billion and American Express's total to $180 billion.

Sources: "The Euromoney/InterSec 250" and "The 75 Largest US Investors," *Euromoney*, September 1987, pp. 365–384; "Global Finance Rankings," *Wall Street Journal*, September 18, 1987, pp. 31D, 32D.

in both loan and capital markets both in their own nations and the Euromarkets. For instance, Deutsche Bank remains a leader in the league of Eurobond managers and continues to dominate the rankings for Deutschemark-denominated Eurobonds.[9] In addition, the German and the French banks have both benefited from favorable tax treatment in amassing reserves against problem loans so that banks in both countries now have loan-loss reserves that are as much as 25 to 50 percent of their exposure—70 percent in the case of Deutsche Bank.[10] This also leads to lower costs when these banks raise new funds because they have higher credit ratings. A number of European banks have a substantial presence in more profitable areas of banking, having been able to enter key markets early due to a lack of restrictions even though they still rely on close relationships with larger industrial firms for a good part of their loan volume. Thus, several of the key international competitors for U.S. banks have put far greater emphasis on higher yield, middle-market and retail loans and on domestic and international capital market activities, although banks with substantial operations in the investment banking business in Europe, acting as market-makers, brokers, and fund managers, were hit especially hard by the October crash, which had less of an impact on U.S. bank operations. The shift to higher yield areas in Europe has marked a major shift away from the asset-building, market share-oriented culture at Banque Nationale de Paris (BNP). At BNP, this shift has been linked to a more customer-driven marketing focus and an improvement in customer services, together with the implementation of a cost-containment program.[11]

Cost of Capital

A second issue for U.S. banks is whether or not their cost of capital is competitive. A quick measure of how difficult it is for banks to raise funds is available from looking at their market to capital ratios, although in the case of nations that permit banks to amass sizable hidden assets, primarily Switzerland and Japan, these estimates can be rather inflated (Table 3.5). But an examination of these values shows that it is much cheaper for banks from Japan, West Germany, and Switzerland to raise money in capital markets than it is for their U.S. competitors. In addition, in a nation such as Japan, because of the government's clear efforts at preserving the growth and stability of the financial sector, it would not be unusual for a bank such as Sumitomo to issue new shares at 50 or even 100 times earnings (its P/E at the end of 1986 was 151) and for the Ministry of Finance to ask other large Japanese banks, such as Mitsubishi Bank or the Industrial Bank of Japan, to buy as much as 20 percent of that issue on their own.

TABLE 3.5
Comparative Market/Book Ratios for International Bank Composites, 1986

Japanese Banks	672.1%
British Clearing Banks	99.6%
Swiss Banks	239.9%
West German Bank	191.0%
U.S. Money Center Banks	89.9%

Source: Thomas H. Hanley et al., "Domestic and International Bank Stock Investing: A Global Approach," Salomon Brothers Inc. Research Department, March 1988, p. 70.

But Japanese banks may face the same pressure as their U.S. counterparts in meeting the proposed capital adequacy requirements. Swiss and German banks, which have been very strongly capitalized for a long time, are unlikely to be forced to make substantial adjustments to meet the new regulations. The new standards that are being established through the work of the Cooke Committee, officially known as the Basle Committee on Banking Regulations and Supervisory Processes of the Bank for International Settlements, will have three parts: redefining bank capital, establishing a capital ratio standard, and creating a new definition and weighting for risk asset capital.[12]

First, a bank's capital is now defined to consist of two tiers. The first tier, capital, is common shareholders' equity, which must be stated net of goodwill by 1992. The second tier, supplementary capital, consists of everything else in a bank's capital structure, such as undisclosed reserves, general loan loss reserves, hybrid capital instruments, subordinated debt, and asset revaluation reserves. But subordinated debt may not be more than half of this secondary capital and loan loss reserves must represent only 1.25 percent of risk-adjusted assets.

In the second part of the agreement, the capital ratio of banks must be set to 7.5 percent of risk-adjusted assets by 1990 and to 8 percent by 1992. Under the agreement, core capital and supplemental capital must each equal 3.625 percent of risk-adjusted assets, and these amounts must be raised to 4 percent each in 1992.

Under the third part of the agreement, each asset on and off the balance sheet is weighted according to broad categories of risk. This means that risk-adjusted assets consist of the sum of the weighted assets of a bank, with some categories being changed considerably. For instance, standby letters of credit and other guarantees, which have been off balance sheet assets but are a direct substitute for credit, will carry a 100 percent weighting, while confirmed credit lines for more than one year will carry a weighting of 50 percent, with the likely consequence that the cost of long-term borrowing will increase.

Several analysts have argued that the impact of these new standards on the Japanese banks will be profound, particularly for the city banks.[13] Their main contention is that regulators from Western nations will be able to use the new standards to force the Japanese to strengthen their regulation of banks, which has permitted Japanese banks to operate in a very undercapitalized manner. The Nomura Research Institute estimates that Japanese banks will need to limit their fundraising to 7,000 billion to 8,000 billion yen (about $60 billion to $70 billion), or else their borrowing will have too great an impact on the ability of other firms to raise funds. If this proves to be true, this will require Japanese banks not only to slow their asset growth but to turn away from their volume-oriented strategy. Apparently this already is happening in Japan, where some branch managers are being instructed to seek higher margin business, such as loans to individuals and small businesses. Also, according to the same report, banks are reducing their system of requiring compensatory balances, noninterest bearing deposits from borrowers who receive loans, but are extending conventional loans with higher rates of interest. In addition, Japanese banks are stepping up their efforts to enter the lucrative securities business and are placing greater emphasis on fee-based services. Finally, the same report also notes that the Ministry of Finance is considering a plan that would allow some of the Japanese city banks to place some of their housing loans in trust funds in order to reduce the size of their outstanding loans.[14]

In my opinion, the Ministry of Finance (MoF) will not let the new standards affect the Japanese banks as much as many analysts contend. Given the MoF's interest in assuring that Japanese banks can compete with their rivals abroad, Japanese banks are likely to get a substantial amount of assistance in adjusting to the new capital rules, such as help in placing their loans in trust funds or through other means. I would even venture to guess that the MoF might help find ways to increase the profitability of the largest banks and securities firms, particularly those that will be leading Japan's efforts in the international market for financial services. Finally, I think that some analysts may be wrong in estimating that only 70 percent of assets are hidden. According to some executives at Japanese banks, the top ten Japanese banks have an average of about 170 percent of assets in their hidden reserves.

In the end, I would argue that the MoF is likely to function in the financial sphere in much the same manner as the Ministry of International Trade and Industry (MITI) has in the industrial sphere. U.S. banks and securities firms need to adjust to a broad new set of competitive realities. But our economic and political structure appears to offer few well-tested mechanisms to promote the adjustment process in a manner that is procompetitive. As has been noted by observers of the U.S. auto industry, including William Abernathy, Kim Clark, and Alan Kantrow, authors of *Industrial Renaissance*, the failure to adjust to a new competitive situation can lead to a lackluster performance in the face of increased pressures from firms that have high levels of manufacturing skills and a great deal of ferment in process and product technology.[15] In banking, the situation is likely to be very similar. The winners in the competitive matchup will be those with the greatest level of banking prowess, including the best innovative and process skills as discussed in the next section.

In short, while I find that many analysts are making valid points about some of the difficulties Japanese banks will face in making needed adjustments, I believe that they underestimate both the role that the MoF is likely to play and the size of the hidden assets that can be drawn upon by the Japanese banks, insurance companies, and securities firms. Although Japanese financial institutions will have to make some adjustments to meet the new capital requirements, I do not believe that they will prove unsurmountable. I would agree with Nozomu Kunishige, an analyst at Citicorp Scrimgeour Vicker, the Tokyo-based stock brokerage owned by Citicorp, who has argued that "in the long run, Japanese banks should become, not only more sound but also more profitable," and likely to be even more formidable competitors for the Western banks in the 1990s than they have been in the 1980s.[16] The only constraint on such political intervention by the MoF would be pressure from the U.S. Treasury and Federal Reserve Board, which could be considerable.

International Dealing Power

The relatively small market capitalization of U.S. financial institutions has led some foreign bankers to conclude that the competitive war is over. They believe that the U.S. financial community has lost the competitive war, largely because the market valuation of its largest institutions no longer compares to that of the largest Japanese and European banks. It remains to be seen, however, whether or not size or "firepower" is being used by foreign competitors to U.S. banks, particularly the Japanese, to develop the innovative skills and expertise necessary to become significant players in innovative products and key financial services. This task is made difficult by the lack of quantitative information.

We know that banks and securities firms have been placing a great deal of emphasis on moving into high-yield operations in banking and improving innovation. But data about such operations are not readily available for banks from the leading nations, be they data on cash management services, deal-making and merger expertise, or skills needed to prepare bond or stock offerings.

Rankings in the Euromarkets can be used to indicate both deal-making sophistication and innovativeness, but those rankings are also influenced by placing power that is closely tied to size of assets, by the financing needs of clients, and by regulatory barriers, such as those that have led Japanese firms to do much of their financing in London in recent years. A clearer indication of relative servicing ability is the personnel cost per employee, since these costs are not as easily inflated by year-to-year special additions as are figures on net income per employee. In addition, a yardstick evaluating innovation and commitment to the development of new technology can be gained by looking at the ranking of banks as clearing firms for correspondents, an activity that depends in large measure on how much banks have invested in communications networks and how well they have managed these networks. Although statistics on daily clearing volume are only available for the domestic operations of U.S. banks, anecdotal information on international clearing networks generally suggests that U.S. banks and securities firms have been far ahead of their foreign counterparts in developing such technologies. While the large Swiss and West German banks have sophisticated international networks, they have used them largely for internal funds transfers.

Data on leaders in Eurobond issues illustrate how quickly Japanese securities firms and banks have risen to the top of global finance. Japanese firms occupied five of the top ten positions in the first half of 1987 compared to none as recently as 1982. Underwriting leadership is especially important for profitability, since managers of issues make twice the fees other syndicate members receive. Still there remain a number of very strong U.S. and European firms at the top of the rankings, including Credit Suisse, First Boston, Deutsche Bank, J.P. Morgan, Salomon Brothers, and SG Warburg of England.[17]

Other Measures of Competitive Strength

Productivity measures should be more sensitive yardsticks of competitive strength. As shown in Table 3.6, Japanese operating expenses in 1986 exceeded those of banks from other nations by nearly two to one, although the Japanese figures may be greatly skewed by the recent rise in the yen. This suggests that although U.S. banks have devoted a great deal of resources to the development of new products, it has not placed a disproportional cost on the money center banks. In addition, if the Japanese and European banks are to move into more lucrative,

TABLE 3.6
Operating Expenses per Employee for Bank Composites, 1986

Bank Composite	Operating Expenses per Employee
U.S. Money Center[1]	$74,680
Japanese[2]	$114,600
Swiss[3]	$74,340
West German[4]	$64,960

[1]12 money center banks
[2]7 largest Japanese banks
[3]The 3 largest Swiss banks
[4]The 3 largest West German banks

Source: Thomas H. Hanley et al., "Domestic and International Bank Stock Investing: A Global Approach," Salomon Brothers Inc. Research Department, March 1988, pp. 91, 98, 107, 117.

TABLE 3.7
Growth in Net Income and Operating Expenses per Employee for International Bank Composites, 1986

Bank Composite	Growth in Net Income Per Employee	Growth in Operating Expenses Per Employee
U.S. Money Center	39%	38%
Japanese*	66%	38%
Swiss	24%	22%
West German**	10%	11%

*Net income from Eigyo-Rieki
**1983–1986

Source: Thomas H. Hanley et al., "Domestic and International Bank Stock Investing: A Global Approach," Salomon Brothers Inc. Research Department, March 1988, pp. 91, 98, 107, 117.

high-yield operations in a manner similar to what has already been done by some U.S. banks, it may impose greater costs than would have been the case during the period of asset growth although many investments in new technology would be capitalized and spread out over a long period of time.

Another interesting finding about productivity as it is usually defined by bank stock analysts, is that cost containment has been similar for both U.S. and Japanese banks. As shown in Table 3.7, operating expenses per employee for both groups of banks grew 38 percent from 1982 to 1986. As expected, cost containment for the West German and Swiss banks was better than among the Japanese and U.S. banks.

While these figures suggest that the Japanese banks' higher operating costs may limit their surge to international prominence, particularly under the new capital requirements, these costs are quite unlikely to offset the big advantage that the Japanese banks have over the other groups of banks in their substantial growth of net income per employee. Table 3.7 shows that Japanese net income per employee grew 66 percent over the 1982 to 1986 period, compared to 39 percent for the U.S. money center banks and 24 percent for the Swiss banks. Such growth in profitability is likely to be inflated by the recent unprecedented rise in the yen. But such profits could enable the Japanese to be more aggressive in their effort to become more competitive internationally. The question remains, however, as to whether this profitability can be maintained as the largest Japanese banks pull back from their asset-growth-based strategy. In addition, Japanese banks may be forced to retreat from offshore short- and medium-term foreign interbank markets, as analysts from Merrill Lynch have claimed, since these markets have smaller returns than those desired by the Ministry of Finance.[18]

Special Strengths of U.S. Financial Institutions

Finally, as noted above, there is extensive anecdotal evidence to suggest that U.S. financial institutions possess the special deal-making and innovative skills to create the financial products and services that will help them to survive the foreign wave of competition. For example, Chase has leveraged its treasury expertise to position the bank as a leader in forward-rate and currency swaps. It also placed fourth in the Euro-commercial paper market, with 62 dealerships in 20 nations. Chase's asset sales network in London, Tokyo, Hong Kong, and nine other places, occupies one of the top three places in global asset sales. Chase is also expanding its "highly regarded" U.S. dollar payment system to foreign markets. This payment system provides Chase with an annuity-like income stream. Income from these and other services, including Chase's global custodial operation with $55 billion under management, has increased by 161 percent during the past two-and-a-half years.[19]

Other major U.S. banks have built up an extremely strong position in merchant banking around the world. Citicorp's merchant banking arm has seats on 28 of the world's stock exchanges and operations in 40 nations. Earnings from merchant banking for 1986 totaled $430 million, or twice the profit levels at First Boston and Morgan Stanley. Nearly 40 percent of this income came from Citicorp's foreign exchange business, the largest in the world, where Citicorp has pioneered the development of hedging and derivative instruments. Citicorp's considerable expertise in swaps and options on foreign exchange transactions allows it to introduce on average about one new foreign exchange product per month.[20] Citicorp, like J.P. Morgan, has already established significant strengths in the European market, handling $200 billion a day in foreign exchange through 100 trading desks in 93 countries, with half the trading in London and the rest evenly split between New York and Tokyo.[21]

Even some of the smaller U.S. banks have used their trading and customer relationships overseas to build skill "niches" with great profitability that may even gain in importance if other U.S. banks retrench from their overseas operations, leaving the remaining ones with enhanced market power. For example, First Chicago clears two-thirds of issuances and payments of Eurodollar certificates of deposit in London, which provides an important opportunity to sell value-added services, such as clearing, custodial, and money transfer services. Globally, First Chicago ranks seventh in foreign exchange and in Tokyo is second to the Bank of Tokyo.[22]

In addition, the largest U.S. banks have developed substantial communications networks. Between 1981 and 1986, they raised the share of their operating expenses for information technology from 10.0 percent to 14.1 percent. At least seven of the leading U.S. banks spent over $200 million a year in information technology in 1986—over $1 billion in Citicorp's case—(see Figures 3.2 and 3.3), while their European rivals were spending about $100 million in the case of Union Bank of Switzerland and about $200 million in the case of Banque Nationale de Paris.[23]

In my opinion, the international networks established by such leading money center banks as J.P. Morgan, Citicorp, and Chase will serve them well during the next phase of competition with their foreign rivals. They provide the scope to enhance deal-making with innovative products and services, the traditional area of strength of the U.S. banks.

Strategic alliances may become another means for firms in the financial services sector to increase profitability, develop a range of services, and improve productivity. One example of such an alliance is the relationship between Credit Suisse and First Boston, the investment bank. While the jointly owned Credit Suisse First Boston has taken on a life of its own in international financial markets,[24] recent discussions between the two firms suggest that Credit Suisse may be considering an alliance to increase its presence in the U.S. market. This would not require a formal takeover but some type of exchange of services and skills, with First Boston gaining access to Credit Suisse's capital base and relationships in Europe. By avoiding some of the complications that would be part of a more formal merger, this arrangement may offer an alternative to foreign banks that want to enter the United States and may suggest new ways

FIGURE 3.2
Expenditures on Information Technology by Seven Leading U.S. Banks, 1986
(in $ billions)

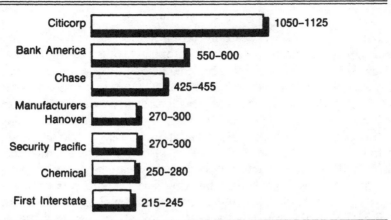

Source: McKinsey and Co. as reproduced in Elizabeth Sowton, "New Target Is Strategic
Databases," in Survey of Information Technology in Finance, *Financial Times* (London),
December 3, 1987, p. 2.

FIGURE 3.3
Expenditures on Information Technology by Large U.S. Commercial Banks, 1981, 1986,
and Projected for 1990 (in $ billions and percentage of operating expenses)

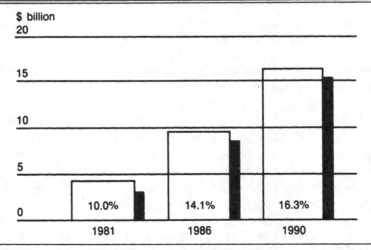

Source: McKinsey and Co. as reproduced in Elizabeth Sowton, "New Target Is Strategic
Databases," in Survey of Information Technology in Finance, *Financial Times* (London),
December 3, 1987, p. 2.

for U.S. financial entities to move abroad under the protective wings of some of the largest foreign banks.

Conclusions

U.S. banks and securities firms face a significant competitive challenge from Japan and from the leading European banks. They must adjust to a new international environment characterized by a weaker dollar, the fact that the United States has become a debtor nation, the fact that America's industrial might is far less than it once was. In short, the U.S. financial community will not be able to draw on the innate strengths of the U.S. economy that helped sustain its rise to global prominence in the past. In addition, U.S. banks will face Japanese banks that have built their assets to such a size that they can begin to play a larger role in providing higher yield banking services and products, and thus challenge U.S. banks in many of their traditional areas of dominance.

But U.S. banks still have a great many strengths. They have lower costs than their Japanese rivals. They have excellent skills in developing innovative financial products. Some of the largest U.S. banks have extensive global networks that enable them to take advantage of high-yield markets. They have emphasized providing high-quality banking services, such as cash management services, clearing, etc., for clients. These advances have improved their competitive position, although their asset size, or "firepower," has certainly declined relative to the Japanese banks.

But Japanese banks may be able to draw on the political power of the Ministry of Finance to enable them to meet new capital adequacy requirements. This would promote their competitiveness in a way similar to the role played by Japan's Ministry of International Trade and Industry in promoting the Japanese auto and semiconductor industries. This political power should not be underestimated.

The MoF will not tell every bank how to compete in global markets. But it is likely to take the lead in resolving problems, helping the Japanese banks to make the necessary adjustments to meet the new international bank capital adequacy requirements. It could also play a pivotal role in facilitating a more aggressive Japanese move into higher-value banking services, such as cash management services, by providing special leasing arrangements for computers and communications equipment and by assisting in the training of bank and computer firm personnel.

By playing such a procompetitive role, the Japanese Ministry could become a model for finance ministries in other nations that want their banks to compete in international financial markets. It could spark a new era of mercantilist policies in service industries more generally, where nations use their political power to assist indigenous service firms to meet challenges in the international markets. Were such a trend to begin, we could see a number of advanced nations establishing competitive strategies for their banking sectors and promoting strategic links or alliances among their banks and those of nations whose banks offered access to expertise and capital as part of such alliances. How should New York respond to the challenge? The seriousness of the competitive threat posed by foreign banks suggests that New York needs to make a careful assessment of how it can enhance the power of its banks to operate as strong international institutions. Such an assessment would include evaluating what would be needed to establish New York as a more international financial center. This assessment has begun through the Governor's Advisory Commission on Financial Services.

The next step is also crucial. For while New York City needs new infrastructure and better policies to promote the growth of financial services, it may also need to develop institutional mechanisms that enable it to respond to global, in addition to regional, competition. Under state and city administrations that are quite sensitive to international financial competition, the governor and senior city officials might take the lead in lobbying for changes in national legislation that are needed to ensure that the city's financial services remain competitive.

Acknowledgment

The author would like to thank Thierry Noyelle of Columbia University and John McPhail of Chase Manhattan for their comments and suggestions.

Notes

1. This argument is made in Richard Wright and Gunter A. Pauli, *The Second Wave: Japan's Global Assault on Financial Services* (New York: St. Martin's Press, 1987).

2. U.S. Congress, Office of Technology Assessment, *International Competition in Services* (Washington, D.C.: U.S. Government Printing Office, July 1987).

3. Robert Heller, Federal Reserve Board, "U.S. Monetary Policy and International Bank Regulation," presented at the World Economic Forum, Davos, Switzerland, January 29, 1988.

4. United Nations Center on Transnational Corporations, "The Role of Transnational Corporations in Services, Including Trans-Border Data Flows: Role of Transnational Banks," February 1, 1988, p. 4.

5. Lawrence W. Cohn et al., "Global Banking Report," Merrill Lynch Capital Markets, Global Securities Research & Economics Group, March 1988, p. 1.

6. Stefan Wagstyl, "BIS Forcing Japan's Banks to Toughen Up," *Financial Times* (London), May 20, 1988, p. 24.

7. Robert Donner and Henry S. Terrell, "The Determinants of the Growth of Multinational Banking Organizations," unpublished manuscript, April 13, 1988.

8. These results are from a proprietary study done by the Management Assistance Corporation of Cambridge, Mass.

9. Thomas Hanley et al., "The Universal Banks of West Germany: Competitive Strategies Begin to Emerge," Salomon Brothers Inc. Stock Research, October 1986, p. 3.

10. Hanley et al., "Universal Banks," p. 21, and Thomas Hanley et al., "European Bank Equity Conference: The Competitive Position of U.S. Multinational Banks in a Global Marketplace," Salomon Brothers Inc. Stock Research, November 1987, p. 16.

11. Hanley et al., "European Bank Equity Conference," pp. 10–11.

12. Cohn, "Global Banking Report," p. 1.

13. Cohn, "Global Banking Report," p. 1; Wagstyl, "BIS"; and David D. Hale, "Cost of Capital, Securitization, and the Growth of Japanese Financial Power," Sumitomo Life Insurance Conference on World Financial Markets, February 1988.

14. Wagstyl, "BIS."

15. William Abernathy, Kim Clark, and Alan Kantrow, *Industrial Renaissance* (New York: Basic Books, Inc., 1983), p. xi.

16. Wagstyl, "BIS."

17. "Credit Suisse First Boston and the International Capital Markets," Harvard Business School Case N9-288-056 (Cambridge: Harvard University, 1988).

18. Cohn, "Global Banking Report," p. 8.

19. Hanley et al., "European Bank Equity Conference," pp. 8–9.

20. Hanley et al., "European Bank Equity Conference," pp. 6–7.

21. Hanley et al., "European Bank Equity Conference," pp. 6–7.

22. Hanley et al., "European Bank Equity Conference," p. 21.

23. Hanley et al., "European Bank Equity Conference," pp. 13, 26.

24. For a history, see "Credit Suisse First Boston and the International Capital Markets."

4

The Regulation
of Global Financial Markets

Richard M. Levich and Ingo Walter

Market and product interpenetration in the international financial service sector has been proceeding at a ferocious rate, driven by rapid financial innovation, securitization of international capital flows, and continued evolution of offshore capital markets. All have induced major competitive and structural changes in the industry and in the competitive positioning of individual financial centers. It is an environment in which countries are rebalancing the static and dynamic efficiency properties against the stability characteristics of their domestic financial systems, and individual institutions are reexamining their corporate strategies and their chances for survival in the competitive environment of the 1990s. And it is an environment in which distortions of competitive conditions have taken on greatly increased importance.

Financial disintermediation and securitization have put ultimate savers and ultimate investors within direct reach of each other through the money and capital markets. Institutions that are in the business of originating, underwriting, and distributing an ever wider range of securities and managing investors' assets have made it possible for individuals, companies, and countries to become increasingly independent of traditional banking relationships. Major corporations have become highly sophisticated financially. Some have developed capabilities to provide in-house the services they formerly bought from banks and securities firms. A few have even penetrated the banking business itself, competing with their old financiers. More will do so in the years ahead.

Banks have fought back. They have moved as fast as they could into the securities business, into financial engineering and consulting services, and into commercial activities such as countertrade and barter. Furthermore market interpenetration has not been confined to national financial systems. The reduced importance of national financial controls, the rapid growth of offshore transactions in the Euromarkets, and the penetration of domestic financial markets by foreign-based institutions have led to a degree of international financial integration where national political boundaries increasingly mean very little.

Public authorities, meantime, recognize the financial efficiency, innovation, and creativity that accompany deregulation. Even governments predisposed to exerting direct control over their financial systems are today rethinking their positions, lest they be left behind in the global financial revolution. The regulators do, of course, express legitimate concerns about financial safety and stability in an industry that has always been susceptible to problems of insolvency, illiquidity, and fraud. The daunting task they face is to design an "optimum" structure of regulation that provides the desired degree of stability at minimum cost to efficiency and financial innovation, and to do so in a way that effectively aligns such policies among banking authorities internationally.

All of this has taken place in an environment of high volatility in interest rates, exchange rates, and inflation rates, creating equal volatility in the real values of assets and liabilities around the world. Volatility means risk. It also means opportunities for profit. Companies exposed to financial risks in various forms, for example, are clearly in the market for products that financial institutions can provide (for a price) to help them control these risks. So are investors, concerned about the durability and purchasing power of their financial assets.

Even without the volatility of recent years, there remain many imperfections in financial markets—for example, the company based in one country that may be able to borrow more cheaply in another, or the investor in one country who may be able to achieve a higher return abroad. Again, financial institutions stand ready to exploit these imperfections for the benefit of their clients and themselves.

The name of the international financial service game today is "value-added"—creating perceived additional value for borrowers and lenders by helping them to manage risks or gain access to financial markets in a way that leaves something on the table for the firm that did the deal. The institutions that will be seen as world-class players during the 1990s are those that have mastered this skill. The supply of financial services on a global scale is a fast-moving, innovative, and fiercely competitive game, one that is unusually vulnerable to competitive distortions imposed on behalf of those players who are not able to keep up.

Financial markets and the financial service sector itself form one of the most structurally complex industries in the world economy. It is also one of the most heavily regulated—owing to the fiduciary nature of much of its activities, its pivotal role in the execution of money and credit policies, as well as its susceptibility to recurring crises. The extensive degree of prudential supervision, regulation, and control covering the financial service sector provides fertile ground for competitive distortions, either in the form of public sector support through protective measures (direct or indirect) or through subsidies and guarantees.

Nevertheless, unlike the rather sad track-record of trade policies in many manufacturing and other service industries (such as insurance), the environment for international trade in financial services—defined as value-added, using factors of production found in one country, which is then sold to residents of another country—has been rather bright. The industry has already become heavily internationalized, and parts of it have become truly globalized, with few prospects that these developments will be reversed in the years ahead.

In this chapter, we examine the changing nature of international financial markets and the financial service industry itself. We begin by surveying developments in international financial markets as a backdrop for a discussion of the sources of real economic gains for financial centers—which are themselves in competition with one another. The chapter continues with an assessment of regulation in this context and concludes with a discussion of the future of New York as a generator of value-added in this sector.

Global Capital Market Developments[1]

One measure of change is the wave of innovation in both financial products and financial markets. The scope of financial innovation can be illustrated by the increase in the variety of products, the volume of trading, and the capitalized value of available securities. The data suggest that a variety of financial markets, which were in their infancy or nonexistent two decades ago, have grown to become major centers of activity and influence. The growth of these markets demonstrates their significance and potential implications for investors, corporate managers, and national policymakers.

Foreign Exchange Markets

The foreign exchange market, the inter-bank market for the exchange of bank deposits denominated in different currencies, has existed in one form or another for centuries. In recent times, the foreign exchange market has been organized as a dispersed, broker-dealer market with high-speed telecommunications systems linking together the various participants in worldwide, 24-hour trading. The volume and efficiency of the market is such that the spread between bid and offer prices in the spot market is often one-tenth of 1 percent, or less, for the major currencies.

Table 4.1 shows the volume of activity in the foreign exchange market and its recent growth. A survey carried out in March 1986 indicated that London was the most active foreign exchange trading location, with transactions totalling $90 billion per day. New York was second, trading $50 billion per day. Tokyo was close behind, with $48 billion per day. Total volume for these three centers was $188 billion per day. Adding the activity from other centers (e.g., Frankfurt, Zurich, Hong Kong, and Singapore), worldwide foreign exchange trading volume possibly exceeded $250 billion per day, or more than $60 trillion per year.[2] With an order flow of this size, many times in excess of world GNP and world trade, the depth and speed of the foreign exchange market is understandable.

For comparison, daily trading volume in New York in 1977 was estimated to be only $5 billion, one-tenth of the estimated volume for 1986. The growth of trading in New York over this period was probably greater than that in London, but not as great as in Tokyo. Nevertheless, worldwide foreign exchange trading clearly grew at a faster pace than other economic aggregates over this ten-year period. The figures for New York also indicate changes in the composition of trading, away from the Canadian dollar and certain European currencies and toward the Japanese yen and Deutsche mark. Note that the Tokyo market is heavily concentrated in yen trading.

Eurocurrencies and Eurobonds

The Eurocurrency market, a market for deposits denominated in a currency different from the indigenous currency of the financial center, began to take shape in the early 1960s. Differential regulation was the principal incentive for the market to take shape. As the cost of particular U.S. banking regulations (i.e., interest rate ceilings on time deposits, mandatory reserve requirements held at zero interest, and mandatory deposit insurance) grew throughout the 1960s, a greater share of banking activity was pushed offshore. The rise of the Eurocurrency market is an example of "unbundling"—in this case, taking the exchange risk of one currency (the U.S. dollar, for example) and combining it with the regulatory climate and political risk of another financial center.

The data in Table 4.2 indicate the growth of the Eurocurrency deposit market, from roughly zero in 1960 to nearly $4.0 trillion on a gross basis and $1.9 trillion on a net basis (netting out all interbank deposits) in June 1987. The market, once exclusively dollar-denominated, has now stabilized to become roughly 70 to 80 percent dollar based, with the currencies of other industrialized countries making up the remainder.

TABLE 4.1
Average Daily Foreign Exchange Trading Volume by Location and Currency, 1986

	Tokyo	London	New York	New York (1977)
Daily Volume, March 1986 (Billions of US $)	$48	$90	$50	$ 5
Percentage Share				
Sterling	—	30	19	17
DM	—	28	34	27
Yen	82	14	23	5
Swiss franc	—	9	10	14
French franc	—	4	4	6
Italian lire	—	2	—	1
Canadian dollar	—	2	6	19
Cross-currency and ECU	—	4	—	—
Dutch guilder	—	—	1	6
Other	18	7	3	5
Total	100%	100%	100%	100%

Source: Joint Survey of the Bank of Tokyo, Bank of England, and the Federal Reserve Bank of New York, March 1986.

TABLE 4.2
Dimensions of the Eurocurrency Deposit Market, 1973–1987 (in $ billions)

Year	Gross Size	Net Size	Eurodollars as % of Gross	U.S. Money Stock (M2)
1973	$ 315	$ 160	74%	861
1974	395	220	76	908
1975	485	255	78	1023
1976	595	320	80	1164
1977	740	390	76	1287
1978	950	495	74	1389
1979	1235	590	72	1498
1980	1525	730	75	1631
1981	1954	1018	79	1793
1982	2168	1152	80	1953
1983	2278	1237	81	2186
1984	2386	1277	82	2374
1985	2846	1480	75	2566
1986	3579	1739	71	2805[a]
1987 (June)	3999	1895	70	N.A.
Compound Growth	20.7%	20.1%	—	9.5%

[a]preliminary

Source: Morgan Guaranty Trust Co., *World Financial Markets*, various issues and *Economic Report of the President*, 1987, Table B-64.

The Eurocurrency market was once small enough to be ignored; today it rivals U.S. financial markets in terms of size and importance. The short-term lending rate in the Eurocurrency market (LIBOR, or London Interbank Offered Rate), determined largely by free-market forces, has become the reference rate for many onshore loan agreements, floating rate notes, and other contracts as well as Euromarket loans.

The Eurobond market developed at approximately the same time as the market for Eurocurrency deposits. Again, differential regulation between offshore and onshore securities activities played a key role in stimulating the development of the market. In 1963, the United States adopted the Interest Equalization Tax (IET), effectively an excise tax on U.S. purchases of new or outstanding foreign stocks and bonds. To no one's surprise, the IET effectively closed foreigners' access to the U.S. bond market; to the surprise of some, the market simply migrated offshore to London and Luxembourg. Other costly U.S. regulations (further international capital controls and a 30 percent withholding tax on interest payments to foreigners) further nurtured the environment for the Eurobond market.

The remarkable growth record of the Eurobond market is presented in Table 4.3. From the first Eurobond floated in 1957, the volume of new offerings reached $6.3 billion in 1972. Two years later, the United States abolished the IET and its capital control program. Eurobond underwritings plunged to $2.1 billion in 1974 and the financial press was anticipating the death of the market. But Eurobonds and U.S. bonds continued to differ in several important ways—investors in Eurobonds paid no withholding tax and held bearer securities, and issuers of Eurobonds avoided costly and time-consuming SEC disclosure requirements. These differences proved to be substantial, and the Eurobond market expanded nearly ninety-fold in the next twelve years. New offerings in the U.S. dollar segment of the market now rival the volume of new corporate bond issues in the United States. The Eurobond market suffered a serious blow in 1987. The depreciation of the U.S. dollar contributed to a decline in Eurodollar bond underwriting, and after the October 1987 market crash investor demand for liquidity also favored domestic government bond markets.

Securitization

The increase in securitization, the tendency for a financial system to channel a greater proportion of its assets through marketable securities bearing market-determined prices rather than through banks, can be seen from a variety of indicators. Both the par value of outstanding publicly traded bonds and the market value of equity capital increased nearly fivefold between 1975 and 1986.[3] Substantial increases in the market value of securities to gross domestic product provide another measure of increasing securitization.

A direct measure of securitization is presented in Table 4.4. Traditionally U.S. nonfinancial corporations have relied heavily on bank loans, a non-traded asset. In 1981 and 1982, bank loans and securitized financing were roughly equal in magnitude. By 1986, more than three-quarters of net new financings were in a securitized form. One explanation for this phenomenon is that for a variety of reasons (but primarily a deterioration in the quality of bank loan portfolios) the credit ratings of banks have fallen relative to their best customers. Corporations have observed that funding costs could be reduced by going directly to the market. As the most creditworthy customers are removed from a bank's portfolio, this trend is reinforced. The trend toward securitization is also reinforced to the extent that investors value liquidity, and are willing to purchase marketable securities at lower yields than a bank might pay on CDs or time deposits.

The trend toward securitization in preference to traditional bank lending is also visible in the international markets. As shown in Figure 4.1, syndicated bank loans captured nearly 60 percent of this market in 1982. In the years since, there has been a steady reduction in syndicated bank lending, along with a steady increase in international bond issues and Euronote programs. The techniques for borrowing through marketable securities are becoming established as one of the routine ways for a corporate treasurer to raise funds.

The final trend that enhances securitization is the transformation of formerly illiquid pools of assets into tradeable securities, using pass-through certificates or collateralized obligations as a structure. Government National Mortgage Association (GNMA), pass-through certificates representing claims on a pool of GNMA-insured mortgages are perhaps the most well-known example, but other federal and private financial institutions began to issue similar certificates in the 1970s. New issues of asset-backed securities reached $269.0 billion in 1986, as reported in Table 4.5. Residential mortgages remain the dominate component of this market. Securities representing commercial mortgages are now available, as well as securities backed by automobile and credit card receivables at the shorter end of the maturity spectrum.

Futures, Options, and Swaps

The extent of financial innovation is perhaps best reflected in a set of new risk management and funding vehicles—futures, options, and swaps—that came into existence in the early 1970s and have experienced

TABLE 4.3
Dimensions of the Eurobond Market, 1970–1987 (in $ billions)

Year	Eurobonds Total	Eurobonds $-denominated	Foreign Bonds	Total International Bond Issues	U.S. Corporate Bond Issues
1970	3.0	—	1.6	4.6	29.0
1971	3.6	—	2.6	6.3	30.1
1972	6.3	3.9	3.4	9.7	25.6
1973	4.2	2.4	3.6	7.8	20.7
1974	2.1	1.0	4.7	6.9	31.5
1975	8.6	3.7	11.3	19.9	42.8
1976	14.3	9.1	18.2	32.5	42.2
1977	17.7	11.6	14.5	32.2	42.3
1978	14.1	7.3	20.2	34.3	20.5
1979	18.7	12.6	22.3	41.0	26.5
1980	24.0	16.4	17.9	41.9	44.6
1981	31.6	26.8	21.4	53.0	38.2
1982	51.6	44.0	26.4	78.0	44.7
1983	48.5	38.4	27.8	76.3	49.5
1984	79.5	63.6	28.0	107.4	59.5
1985	136.7	97.8	31.0	167.8	86.3
1986	188.7	119.1	39.4	228.1	113.5[a]
1987[b]	140.5	56.7	36.8	177.3	N.A.
Compound Growth[c]	29.5%	27.6%	22.0%	27.6%	6.2%

[a]first three quarters at annual rate
[b]through end of October, not annualized
[c]through end of 1986

Source: Morgan Guaranty Trust Co., *World Financial Markets,* various issues and *Economic Report of the President,* 1987, Table B-90.

TABLE 4.4
Net Borrowing by U.S. Nonfinancial Corporations, 1981–1986 (in $ billions)

	1981	1982	1983	1984	1985	1986
Securitized Financing	45.0	37.7	27.2	78.4	90.5	98.6
Corporate Bonds	28.1	44.2	24.6	55.3	77.0	90.5
Open Market Paper	16.9	−6.5	2.6	23.1	13.5	8.1
Bank Loans	43.5	39.7	18.0	77.0	35.5	27.1
Ratio of Securitized Financing to Bank Loans	1.03	0.95	1.51	1.02	2.55	3.64

Source: Salomon Brothers, Inc., "Prospects for Financial Markets in 1987," New York, December 1986, p. 55.

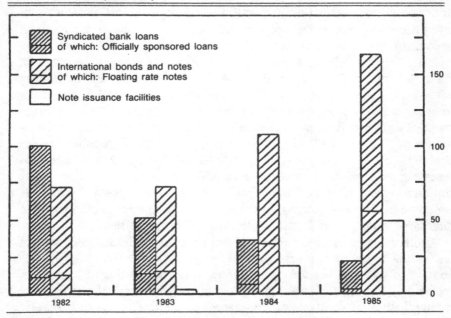

FIGURE 4.1
International Borrowing Through Syndicated Bank Loans Versus Tradeable Bonds and Notes, 1982–1985 ($ billions)

Source: Bank for International Settlements, *Annual Report,* 1986.

TABLE 4.5
Gross New Issues of Asset-Backed Securities, Selected Years (in $ billions)

	1980	1982	1984	1985	1986[a]	1987[b]
Residential Mortgage	22.0	55.0	66.7	114.0	253.3	217.0
Commercial Mortgage	—	—	1.3	6.0	5.6	7.0
Automobile Receivables	—	—	—	—	10.0	15.0
Credit Card Receivables	—	—	—	—	.05	1.0
Total	22.0	55.0	68.0	120.0	269.0	240.0

[a]Estimate
[b]Forecast

Source: Salomon Brothers, Inc., "Prospects for Financial Markets in 1987," New York, December 1986, p. 55.

extraordinary growth. Their importance lies beyond what the numerical entries may suggest.[4] The aggregate open interest in financial futures and options, a measure of the speculative capital at risk in the market, rose to $680 billion at the end of September 1986, an increase of nearly 75 percent over the year-end 1985 figure. Open interest, as reported in Table 4.6, is split roughly two-to-one between futures contracts and options contracts. Futures and options written against contracts on interest-bearing securities account for the greatest open interest, 94 percent in the case of futures and 67 percent in the case of options.

Daily trading volume for futures and options contracts, reported in Table 4.7, mirrors the above findings. The dominant share of trading volume is in interest-rate contracts, more so in the case of futures than in options. And among contracts on interest bearing securities, the three-month Eurodollar futures contract is by far the most popular, accounting for about 75 percent of all activity. The three-month Eurodollar futures contract currently trades roughly 50,000–75,000 contracts per day, representing an aggregate face value of $50–$75 billion. The Eurodollar contract is useful for hedging LIBOR interest rate exposure, which as we noted earlier, has become the major reference rate for pricing variable rate bank lending and floating rate note (FRN) securities.[5]

Another indicator of the potential impact of financial futures markets on trading behavior is illustrated in Figure 4.2, which graphs the daily volume of treasury bond futures trading and the volume of trading in the underlying cash market. The data clearly show that the volume of trading in futures contracts now swamps the volume in the cash market by a factor of four. A similar ratio maintains between trading volume in stock index futures and underlying equity shares.

The development of financial futures markets has spread around the world (see Table 4.8). This clearly represents new competition for U.S. futures markets, but it also has helped to supplement the trend toward 24-hour trading in major financial instruments, such as Eurodollar futures and Deutsche marks. Figure 4.3 illustrates 24-hour trading of U.S. Treasury bonds in the New York, London, and Tokyo cash markets. Treasury bond futures are traded in Chicago, London, Sydney, and Singapore. Active offshore trading in these futures has driven Chicago to introduce evening trading (6:00–9:00 P.M., Chicago time) to recapture some of the volume.

Maximizing Real-Sector Benefits: Financial Centers

Where are the aforementioned activities carried out and the real economic benefits created? While one major element of the theory of

TABLE 4.6
Aggregate Open Interest in Major World Financial Futures and Options Contracts, Selected Years (in $ billions)

	1975	1980	1984	1985	1986:3
Futures	0.2	81.0	190.7	253.7	439.9
Interest Rate Contracts	0.0	78.8	182.1	236.0	412.4
Bonds	0.0	35.9	25.0	49.5	104.3
Money Market	0.0	42.9	157.1	186.5	308.1
Stock Index Contracts	0.0	0.0	4.6	9.7	18.1
Currencies	0.2	2.2	4.0	8.0	9.4
Options	0.0	0.0	40.3	138.2	239.6
Interest Rate Contracts	0.0	0.0	21.5	88.8	161.9
Bonds	0.0	0.0	21.5	41.4	45.8
Money Market	0.0	0.0	0.0	47.4	116.1
Stock Index Contracts	0.0	0.0	14.7	37.1	38.9
Currencies	0.0	0.0	4.1	12.3	38.8
Aggregate Open Interest[a]	0.2	81.0	231.0	391.9	679.5

[a]Measured by dollar par or index value of outstanding positions on the last day of the period.

Source: Salomon Brothers, Inc., "Prospects for Financial Markets in 1987," New York, December 1986, p. 23.

TABLE 4.7
Aggregate Daily Trading Volume in Major World Financial Futures and Options Contracts, Selected Years (in $ billions)

	1975	1980	1984	1985	1986:3
Futures	0.0	25.3	55.1	86.0	134.6
Interest Rate Contracts	0.0	24.2	46.7	73.4	115.9
Bonds	0.0	6.0	11.9	25.7	57.9
Money Market	0.0	18.2	34.8	47.7	58.0
Stock Index Contracts	0.0	0.0	5.5	8.9	14.4
Currencies	0.0	1.1	2.9	3.7	4.3
Options	0.0	0.0	8.2	24.5	34.4
Interest Rate Contracts	0.0	0.0	1.9	11.5	16.3
Bonds	0.0	0.0	1.9	6.5	6.7
Money Market	0.0	0.0	0.0	5.0	9.6
Stock Index Contracts	0.0	0.0	6.0	12.3	15.6
Currencies	0.0	0.0	0.3	0.7	2.5
Aggregate Trading Volume[a]	0.0	25.4	63.2	110.5	169.0

[a]Daily average of the dollar par or index value of transactions.

Source: Salomon Brothers, Inc., "Prospects for Financial Markets in 1987," New York, December 1986, p. 23.

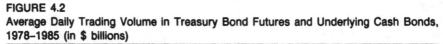

FIGURE 4.2
Average Daily Trading Volume in Treasury Bond Futures and Underlying Cash Bonds,
1978–1985 (in $ billions)

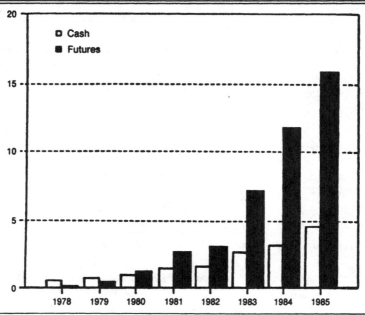

Source: First Boston Corporation, *Handbook of Securities of the United States Government
and Federal Agencies*, 1986, p. 225.

finance focuses on the real-sector benefits of financial markets (i.e.,
transfers of funds from savers to investors, inter-temporal smoothing of
consumption, channeling funds into their most productive use, providing
liquidity and risk transfer services, and so forth), most of the literature
ignores the geographic aspects. In his monograph on "The Formation
of Financial Centers," Kindleberger analyzes the forces leading to the
rise and fall of both national and international financial centers. The
basic dichotomy is between those forces favoring centralization versus
those leading to decentralization.[6]

National Financial Centers

Clearing of interregional payments was an important force leading to
centralization of a national banking system. Analogous to a modern
"hub-and-spoke" airline system, it was far more efficient for bank transfers
to be cleared multilaterally through a single locality than for each bank
to clear payments bilaterally with all other banks in the system. Given
the development of such an efficient system for payments, firms found
that centralization helped them to economize on working capital balances.

TABLE 4.8
World Futures Exchanges

Futures Markets in the United States	Year Founded	Principal Types of Contracts			
		Physical	Currencies	Interest Rates	Index
Chicago Board of Trade (CBT)	1848	•		•	•
Chicago Mercantile Exchange (CME)	1919	•	•	•	
Coffee, Sugar, and Cocoa Exchange (New York)	1882	•			•
Commodity Exchange, Inc. (COMEX) (New York)	1933	•			
Kansas City Board of Trade (KCBT)	1856	•			•
Mid-America Commodity Exchange (Chicago)	1880	•	•	•	
Minneapolis Grain Exchange	1881	•			
New York Cotton Exchange, Inc.	1870	•	•		•
Citrus Associates of the New York Cotton Exchange	1966	•			
Petroleum Associates of the New York Cotton Exchange	1971	•			
New York Futures Exchange (NYFE)	1979				•
New York Mercantile Exchange	1872	•			
Chicago Rice and Cotton Exchange	1976	•			
Principal Foreign Futures Markets					
International Futures Exchange (INTEX) (Bermuda)	1984	•			•
Bolsa de Mercadorios de Sao Paulo	1917	•			
London International Financial Futures Exchange (LIFFE)	1982		•	•	•
Baltic International Freight Futures Exchange BIFFEX (London)	1985				•
Tokyo Financial Futures Exchange	1985		•	•	•
Singapore International Monetary Exchange SIMEX (Singapore)	1984		•	•	•
Hong Kong Futures Exchange	1977	•			•
New Zealand Futures Exchange	1985	•	•	•	
Sydney Futures Exchange	1960	•	•	•	•
Toronto Futures Exchange	1984		•	•	•
Kuala Lumpur Commodity Exchange	1985*	•			

*Reorganized after default.

Source: *The Wall Street Journal, Futures Magazine, Intermarket Magazine,* various issues, and Chicago Mercantile Exchange, *1985 Annual Report,* as cited in Robert Colb, *Understanding Futures Markets* (New York: Scott Foresman, 1988).

FIGURE 4.3
U.S. Treasury Bond Futures Trading Hours (Chicago Time)

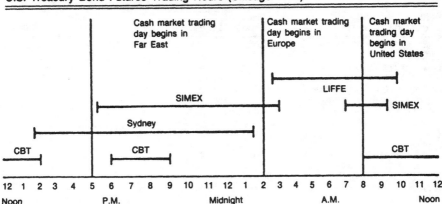

Source: *Futures Magazine*, March 1987 as cited in Robert Colb, *Understanding Futures Markets* (New York: Scott Foresman, 1988).

Scale economies gave banks at the financial center a pricing advantage in lending.

Centralization also plays a role in securities markets as well as in banking. Centralization reduces the costs of searching for the most favorable execution prices, which improves the informational efficiency of the market. Centralization also lowers the transaction costs of securities transfers and increases the scale of operations which benefits liquidity.

But other forces in the economy favor decentralization of financial centers. First, costly information about local borrowers, small firms, and local market conditions points to the need for face-to-face contact and decentralized operations. Even though information costs have been reduced through standardized credit tools and communication costs have been dropping, there is still a need for regional financial centers. Second, national time zone differences (e.g., New York versus Los Angeles) impose another diseconomy from centralization. Asking one or both parties in a transaction to work during non-normal business hours represents another cost of centralized operations. A third factor favoring decentralization is risk—exposure to local tax laws, regulations, and the local business cycle favors decentralized financial firms.

After weighing these various factors, Kindleberger concludes that "Up to a certain degree of concentration, positive externalities and economies of scale appear to outweigh diseconomies, favoring centralization."[7]

Identifying which locality would become the financial center of a nation poses a complex problem. Kindleberger draws attention to nine factors:[8]

- central bank
- culture
- tradition
- economies of scale
- central location
- administrative capital
- transport
- national and local policies
- corporate headquarters

All have played some part in the formation of European and American financial centers. The linkages between these factors and the location of a financial center are inexact.

International Financial Centers

The same process that tends to lead to a single dominant financial center within a country has also tended to favor the emergence of a single worldwide financial center with "the highly specialized functions of lending abroad and serving as a clearinghouse for payments among countries.[9] The principal difference in the international case is that exchange risk and higher transaction costs are formidable barriers that prevent as high a degree of centralization. International time-zone differences are obviously more extreme than in any one country, and (other factors held constant) residents would prefer to transact within their own time zone. Exposures to risk (through national tax laws, national business cycles, and so forth) are greater across countries than within them and favor decentralization.

Again, the identity of the international financial center(s) depends in a complex way on a set of factors including (in addition to the nine cited above) the international prominence of the national currency and the international investment position of the nation. In the Eighteenth Century, the Dutch reached the pinnacle of "bankers to the world." The formation of the British Empire elevated London to the international financial center of the world. At the end of World War I, the United States ceased being an international debtor, but it was not until the formation of the Bretton-Woods system that the United States and the U.S. dollar were firmly established as the key country and key currency in the international financial system.

In an age when national policymakers are held accountable for domestic economic performance, the decision to assume the duties of an international financial center has a strategic policy dimension. Kindleberger has argued that between World War I and the Tripartite Monetary

Agreement of 1936, the international monetary system lacked effective leadership.[10] In his view, the Depression was a result of an ineffective transition in which "an old center (London) lost the capacity to serve as the center of the world financial system, and the most promising candidate for the position (New York) was unwilling or unable to fulfill the responsibilities."[11]

In more modern times, we have observed one country (England) withdraw its currency (the Pound sterling) from international reserve currency status, while other countries (Germany, Japan, and Switzerland) have actively discouraged the internationalization of theirs. A number of smaller countries (Luxembourg, Singapore, and the Bahamas) have actively encouraged the development of offshore banking centers in their countries, presumably for its positive impact on development. And because of the footloose nature of the financial services industry, many countries have organized and promoted financial futures and options markets to compete with the well-established markets in the United States (Table 4.8).

Developments now in progress suggest that we are unlikely to see a single dominant international financial center in the decades ahead. The United States has lost its preeminence as the mature creditor country of the world, and the role of the U.S. dollar as a unit of account, a medium of exchange, and a store of value is in decline. Japan is the world's largest creditor nation and the Japanese have liberalized the use of the yen as well as the structure of Japanese financial markets. While Germany and Switzerland have strongly resisted a larger international role for their currencies, the coming harmonization of the European Economic Community in 1992 may launch the Deutsche mark (or the European Currency Unit) into an international role. The fast-paced development of numerous Pacific Basin countries, as well as China and India (among others) suggest that economic power will be distributed more evenly in the future than it has been in the recent past.

In the next decade, it seems likely that some type of tripartite arrangement will develop to guide international monetary relations and that (because of reduced communications and information costs) the system may be able to tolerate multiple and geographically dispersed international financial centers. But it also seems likely that the existing financial centers and exchanges, with their advantages of overwhelming size and liquidity, should be able to maintain their relative positions.

Benefits to a Financial Center

Within the context of metropolitan development and growth, finance stands at the apex as the most (geographically) concentrated of services provided for the rest of the nation. Finance is invariably more concentrated (geographically) than commerce, industry, or transport. The comparative advantage of cities is the speed with which face-to-face transactions, especially those in which there is considerable uncertainty, can take place. The history of the New York financial market is well-documented and supports the notion that financial institutions developed around an active port and wholesaling operations. In turn, ancillary commercial activities (such as printers and hotels) developed and corporate head-quarters were attracted.

The benefits of a financial center are a function of the value-added produced by the factors of production (labor and capital) employed by the financial institutions. The value-added will be greatest where the skill levels are highest and the linkages to ancillary commerce are highest. At the low end of the scale, financial centers such as Panama and the Cayman Islands serve as booking centers to take advantage of liberal tax laws and offshore regulations. They provide employment opportunities where the opportunity cost for labor is likely to be small. Moving upscale, Luxembourg has advanced from a simple tax haven to a re-invoicing center and a center for Eurobond activities. Singapore was predominantly an offshore deposit-taking center that now has a niche as an active financial futures exchange.

Clearly, the most value-added lies in the skill-intensive and capital-intensive activities of financial institutions—market-making, underwriting, risk management, product development, mergers and acquisitions, provision of liquidity services, and so forth. These are the most highly remunerated activities that because of the need for physical proximity are likely to take place in the financial center.

An analysis of the direct benefits to cities or nations from the financial services industry is beyond the scope of this discussion. However, in most cases, we would assume that a larger volume of issuing, trading, and other financial activity should correspond to greater benefits to the community.

One counter-example is the case of foreign exchange. Table 4.9 reports the number of banks and traders engaged in foreign exchange trading. The figures for London are roughly twice those for New York—roughly similar to relative trading volume figures shown earlier in Table 4.1. But the table also reveals that Western Europe has more than three times as many banks and traders involved in foreign exchange trading as does North America. The interpretation of these numbers is not completely clear. Obviously with more countries, currencies and trade in Western Europe, there are more trading rooms and traders. This may transfer gains to European banks that provide those services, but it may

TABLE 4.9
Number and Location of Banks and Traders in Foreign Exchange, 1983, 1985

Location	1983		1985	
	Banks	Traders	Banks	Traders
North America				
New York	96	667	108	793
Toronto	12	96	18	120
Chicago	14	84	14	81
San Francisco	8	52	7	43
Los Angeles	8	38	11	46
Total	138	929	158	1,083
Western Europe				
London	227	1,645	258	1,603
Luxembourg	68	356	74	353
Paris	64	378	75	459
Zurich	30	199	35	245
Frankfurt	47	300	48	334
Milan	35	212	37	191
Brussels	29	186	33	201
Total	500	3,276	560	3,386
Asia/Middle East				
Tokyo	27	150	30	169
Singapore	49	234	69	293
Hong Kong	54	246	52	306
Bahrain	26	106	38	173
Total	156	736	189	941

Source: Hambros Bank, *Foreign Exchange and Bullion Dealers Directory* (London: 1983 and 1985).

also represent a net loss of efficiency for a region that operates with multiple currencies rather than as a unified currency area.

The Regulatory Dimension

Banking and finance are highly sensitive sectors. Despite careful diversification in asset deployment, exposures incurred in lending activities always involve solvency risk while asset-liability management must constantly deal with liquidity risk and interest rate risk. The very role of financial intermediation entails the assumption of such risks. Moreover, fraud, misrepresentation, financial collapse, predatory behavior, self-dealing, bubbles, busts, and shocks have afflicted the U.S. financial system over the centuries, as they have elsewhere in the world.

Prudential Control

Governments are well aware of the inherent risks and potential conflicts involved in domestic banking, securities underwriting, trading and dealing in financial instruments, foreign exchange, precious metals, and the like. Most notably in banking, these risks focus on the solvency of borrowers and the liquidity of institutions that are highly geared. Banking crises always carry with them negative externalities—damage imposed on individuals and institutions outside the firms directly involved and, in some cases, outside the industry itself. It is conventional wisdom that major banking crises can lead to severe damage to employment, income, economic growth, and related goals of society.

In order to protect themselves against such adverse external consequences, therefore, countries have built elaborate "safety net" systems that are designed to provide liquidity to institutions in trouble, insure depositors, and sometimes bail out borrowers to help the bank maintain solvency. The operation of domestic financial safety nets invariably creates problems of efficiency and fairness; for example, how to distinguish between institutions that are TBTF (too big to fail) and those TSTS (too small to save), and how to neutralize competitive distortions that may result from people's expectations about the operation of the safety net.[12] Even more important, the existence of a safety net creates potential "moral hazard" problems where management of financial institutions, knowing that they are likely to be bailed out, will behave in a less risk-averse manner and thus impose substantial contingent liabilities on those who hold up the safety net—the taxpayers and the general public.

To cope with this problem, and to ensure the safety and stability of national financial systems, governments apply various techniques of financial surveillance and control, ranging from careful bank-examination procedures, reserve requirements, mandatory asset ratios and maximum lending limits to risk-related deposit insurance premiums, disclosure provision, securities laws, and moral suasion. Countries deal with this problem in different ways. Some simply nationalize all or major parts of the domestic financial services industry. Regulation and control usually damages the efficiency of the domestic financial system, but this loss in efficiency can be considered as something of an "insurance premium" and is usually considered to be more than offset by the resulting gain in the safety and stability of the system.

Deregulation: Gains and Costs

Deregulation in financial services has become a fact of life in the United States. Information and transactions costs are falling. New competitors are entering the financial services field, while others seek exit or combine with viable players as elegantly as possible. New financial products come on-stream almost daily, their number and variety limited only by the human imagination. Artificial barriers to competition, some of which have been in place for decades, are being subjected to steady erosion. Competitors bid actively for human as well as financial resources, even as product, process, applications, management, and marketing technologies evolve faster than ever before. In short, an environment of vigorous competition exists, based on concepts like institutional competitive advantage, specialization, economies of scale, and economies of scope.

If the process is permitted to work itself out, a far stronger and more efficient national financial system will eventually evolve, where excess profits ultimately disappear, transactions costs are driven to a bare minimum, information becomes much more readily available, the basis for rational decision-making improves, and only the fittest competitors are able to prosper for very long.

If deregulation is to be justified in economic terms, that justification must come in large part through substantive change in competitive performance in the provision of corporate financial services. Glass-Steagall notwithstanding, there is already substantial competition between investment banks and commercial banks for a wide variety of such services, as well as in the international capital market. In areas where there has been an absence of artificial barriers to competition, the degree of efficiency and innovation that characterizes the various competing financial services firms has been very high indeed, with commensurate benefits accruing directly to the users of the services and more broadly to the economic and financial system as a whole.

If there are potential benefits associated with the deregulation of corporate financial services in the United States, there are also potential costs with respect to both economic efficiency and equity dimensions. Potential costs include lessened stability of the financial system and the exploitation of conflicts of interest on the part of financial institutions engaged.

Each financial crisis in recent years, including the stock market collapse of October 19th, 1987, has brought with it a tightening of supervision and control under existing statutes, but no major moves toward re-regulation. In this way, even major shocks have been absorbed relatively smoothly without incurring losses in the system's core efficiency and dynamism. Indeed, the case for continued deregulation has in some ways been strengthened if it fosters greater activity diversification and earnings stability on the part of the most viable, best-managed players in banking as well as securities markets.

Thus while financial regulation is necessary to ensure the stability and soundness of the financial system, it invariably generates efficiency losses. At the level of the firm, regulation constrains management's freedom in deploying the institution's capital and human resources, in designing financial and organizational structures, and in developing business strategies. At the level of society, regulation may foster a misallocation of resources, reduced innovation and international competitiveness, and constrain the contribution of the financial system to economic growth. In a dynamic world, national policymakers must continuously monitor the cost-benefit trade-off in financial regulation.

International Competitive Impact of Regulation

The preceding section reviewed numerous features of financial regulation and deregulation, both of which may contribute net benefits to society. It will be useful for our analysis in this section to think of financial regulation as a tax on the financial services industry. Two points on applying the infamous "Laffer curve" in this context are clear—with a zero tax rate, there are zero tax revenues (i.e., no safeguards beyond those that the private market provides for itself), and with a 100 percent tax rate, there are also no tax revenues, because no financial services are provided privately. While regulations might be designed to maximize tax revenues, we will argue that this is not an appropriate policy objective. The goal of policy should be to balance the level of regulatory control versus deregulatory freedom in order to optimize the welfare of society—to achieve the highest levels of productive output with acceptable levels of risk emanating from the financial sector.

Even within a single economy, the optimal design of financial regulation is a complex matter. Thinking of regulation as a tax, the issue we wish to consider is whether a government will necessarily be able to collect a tax that is "excessive." Regulations (e.g., reserve requirements, capital adequacy requirements, and so forth) impose costs which, in part, will be transferred to clients.

Costly regulations create incentives for financial firms to innovate in order to reduce their costs and capture a larger market share. Money market mutual funds and off-balance sheet financing techniques are two well-known domestic examples. The greater the extent of regulatory costs, the greater is the incentive to innovate or avoid the domestic financial system. The movement of Citibank's credit card operations from New York to South Dakota (in part, to escape New York's interest rate ceilings) illustrates this kind of domestic mobility. The limiting case might be found in a country experiencing hyperinflation, in which case residents may shift into commodity monies or completely avoid domestic financial institutions.

In the international setting, the scope for governments to collect excessive regulatory taxes is reduced because there is greater competition among national regulatory environments. Each domestic financial center faces competition from foreign and offshore financial centers. As transactions costs and information costs decline, the cost of using an offshore financial center declines. The development of offshore currency and bond markets in the 1960s (discussed earlier) represents a case in which borrowers and lenders found that they could carry out the requisite market transactions more efficiently and with sufficient safety by operating offshore—in a parallel market. Capital flight from LDCs is an extreme example of residents escaping the local inflationary tax or fleeing from low or highly variable real rates of return.

Our main point here is that in today's world, communications costs are low and capital mobility is high. It is becoming less feasible for a state or a nation to impose a net regulatory burden that stands too far apart from world norms.

In the past, however, policymakers have often set financial regulations as if there would be no international feedback effects. As discussed earlier in this chapter, reserve requirements and Regulation Q interest rate ceilings (in conjunction with a high interest rate environment) gave a strong incentive for the development of Eurocurrency markets. The United States did not participate in the development of this market. It was only in 1981 that International Banking Facilities permitted a quasi-off-shore market (open only to nonresidents) in the United States. Other U.S. regulations such as the Interest Equalization Tax (1963), the Voluntary Foreign Credit Restraint Program (1968), withholding taxes on interest payments to foreigners (dropped in July 1984), and the time-consuming SEC registration process (modified in 1982 with Rule 415 on shelf registration) all gave strong incentives for the development of the Eurobond market.[13] Even the U.S. Treasury offered four "targeted Treasury issues" to the Eurobond market in an effort to lower its funding costs.

In the last 20 years, U.S. financial institutions have moved a substantial part of their operations offshore, suggesting that they judged the cost of domestic financial regulations excessive. If we assume that transaction costs and communication costs are declining, would it follow that the "equilibrium regulatory tax" on financial institutions is zero, i.e., that a financial institution would migrate rather than pay any positive regulatory tax?

In our judgment, a long-run equilibrium can be maintained with a *positive* regulatory tax. Financial transactions involve uncertainty—about the monetary unit of account, about the credit worthiness of the financial institutions, and about the political stability of the financial center. Financial institutions ought to value their access to lender of last resort facilities, the opportunity to be headquartered in a stable political climate, and so forth. And in those markets that are largely unregulated, namely the Eurocurrency and Eurobond markets, financial institutions overall have behaved prudently in order to maintain the long-term value of their franchises. If financial institutions find it in their interest to pay some regulatory tax, the economic question then concerns the sustainable magnitude of this tax.

As we have stressed throughout, communications costs are falling and capital mobility is increasing. Whatever the cost of the regulatory burden placed on financial institutions, it seems clear that this cost must be roughly similar across the major countries of the world. Given the complexity of the financial system, accomplishing the necessary consistency, coverage, and coordination of regulations represents a major undertaking. The approach to regulation in the Eurocurrency market provides some indication of the problems that might be faced and how they might be overcome.[14]

Eurocurrency operations occur "offshore" but not beyond the reach of governments. Eurocurrency banks could be regulated on a "territorial" basis. Under this approach, the country in which a deposit was created would impose reserve requirements on both domestic banks as well as branches and subsidiaries of foreign banks. For the territorial approach to be effective, an agreement among all countries, small and large, that might potentially harbor Eurobanks would be required. On the other hand, all of the major players in this market are headquartered in a major industrial country—this is almost a criterion for success in attracting deposits in this market. Eurocurrency banks could instead be regulated on a "domiciliary" approach requiring the country in which the headquarters of the bank is domiciled to impose consistent regulations across all offshore branches and subsidiaries. The latter approach would "only" require agreement across major industrial countries. A large bank might move its headquarters to a regulation-free mini-state, but this seems unlikely given inter alia the value of lender of last resort facilities, as argued earlier.

The approach taken by the Bank for International Settlements (BIS) is along the lines of the domiciliary approach. In the Basle Concordat (1974), the United States and 30 other countries agreed to assume lender of last resort responsibility for their offshore banks. In 1980, the BIS announced an agreement among central banks requiring commercial banks headquartered within their territories to consolidate their worldwide accounts. This agreement would enable bank examiners to regulate offshore and onshore operations on a consistent basis.

The recent discussions at the BIS on capital adequacy requirements fit within the domiciliary framework. A recent study by Cumming and Sweet suggests that there is considerable variation in the financial structures across the world's major financial markets, with greater integration of banking and securities activities outside of Japan and the United States.[15] Whether the present level of diversity is consistent with stable financial markets is unclear. We can conclude that the "one-market" hypothesis outlined in the Brady Commission Report and elsewhere clearly needs to be interpreted internationally. Not only are there strong arbitrage price linkages between stocks, futures, options, and various "bank products" within one country, but these linkages extend between countries for similar products denominated in U.S. dollars or in other currencies. A consistent set of regulations will be necessary to prevent competitive distortions, which are the topic of the next section.

Competitive Distortions

The C-A-P Matrix

To understand how competitive distortions arise, it is useful to turn first to an analysis of how firms operate across international markets. To do so, it is useful to visualize these markets as combining three principal dimensions.[16]

- Client (C-dimension)
- Arena (A-dimension)
- Product (P-dimension)

Figure 4.4 depicts these dimensions in the form of a matrix comprised of C × A × P cells. Individual cell characteristics can be analyzed in terms of conventional competitive-structure criteria. The inherent attractiveness of each cell depends on the size of the prospective risk-adjusted returns that can be extracted from it. The durability of its attractiveness will depend on the ability of new players to enter the cell and the development of substitute products over time. The cells themselves are linked with the respect to institutional competitive performance through economies of scale and economies of scope.

The ability of financial institutions to exploit profit opportunities within the C-A-P matrix depends on a number of key firm-specific attributes. These include the adequacy of the institution's capital base and its institutional risk base, its human resources, its access to information and markets, its technology base and managerial culture, and the entrepreneurial qualities of its people.

FIGURE 4.4
Trade Barriers in the International Financial Services Activity Matrix

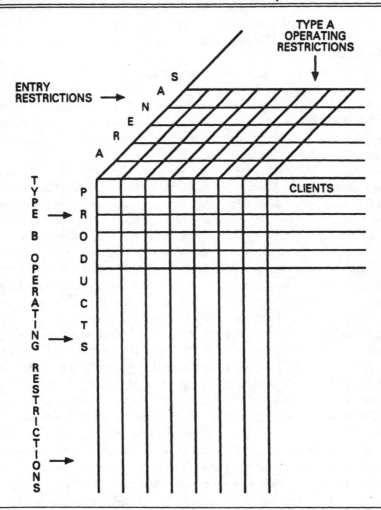

Source: Ingo Walter, *Global Competition in Financial Services* (Cambridge, Mass.: Ballinger–Harper & Row, 1988).

Firms in the international financial services industry are obviously sensitive to incremental competition in C-A-P cells, where natural entry barriers are limited. Market penetration by foreign-based competitors—especially in the wholesale and capital markets end of the business—can erode indigenous players' returns and raise protectionist motivations. Given the economic interests involved, banks and other financial institutions are in an excellent position to convert them into political power in order to achieve protection. They are often exceedingly well connected politically, and their lobbying power motivated by protectionist drives can be awesome.

The U.S. Treasury, OECD, Walter, and Sagari have undertaken extensive surveys of restrictions that are imposed on foreign-based banks and other firms in the financial services industry.[17] These take the form of entry barriers, operating restrictions that affect access to client groups (Type A), and operating restrictions affecting the ability to supply the market with specific products (Type B).

In terms of Figure 4.4, *entry* barriers restrict the movement of financial services firms in the lateral "arenas" dimension of the matrix. A firm that is blocked out of a particular national market faces a restricted lateral opportunity set that excludes the relevant tranche of "client" and "product" cells. Windows of opportunity, created by countries relaxing entry barriers, often trigger an enthusiastic response on the part of institutions envisioning potential super-normal returns in some of the previously inaccessible cells. Firms facing entry barriers may nevertheless be able to gain access to particular cells in the restricted tranche by transferring the actual transaction to a different arena, e.g., one of the Euromarket functional or booking centers or the institution's home country.

Once having gained access to a particular arena, *operating restrictions* constrain either the depth of service a foreign-based financial institution can supply to a particular cell (e.g., lending limits, staffing limits, restrictions on physical location) or in the feasible set of cells within the tranche (e.g., limits on services foreign banks are allowed to supply and the client groups they are allowed to serve). As noted in Figure 4.4, operating restrictions can be subclassified in terms of whether they place limits on the kinds of financial services that may be sold locally (Type A) or the specific client-groups that may be served (Type B). Operating limits may severely reduce profitability associated with the arena (country) concerned for foreign-based players, while creating significant excess returns for the protected industry.

Besides applying entry and operating restrictions to foreign-based players, regulators may tolerate a certain amount of anti-competitive, cartel-like behavior on the part of domestic institutions. In attempting to gain significant market-share with "sensitive" client groups, obtaining funding in the local currency market, placing securities with domestic investors, and obtaining underwriting mandates, foreign firms intruding into the national marketplace may be stepped-on by indigenous players, with the authorities turning a blind eye to the implications for the industry's competitive performance.

At the same time, economies of scope and scale may be significantly constrained by entry and operating restrictions in a particular market. In both cases, the importance of the link between competitive distortions and horizontal integration in the international financial services industry is clear. At the same time, correspondent relationships with local banks represent an alternative for sharing in the returns associated with the blocked cells, particularly with respect to international trade, foreign exchange, syndications, and other wholesale transactions.

The strategic implications of barriers to trade in financial services thus seem clear. They reduce the feasibility set within the C-A-P matrix; they place a premium on windows of opportunity; they increase the importance of horizontal linkages and the assessment of their value to a financial institution's international strategy; and they raise the importance of lobbying activity to open up markets where cells having potentially super-normal returns are blocked or restricted, and to keep them that way when barriers to competition are the source of excess returns.

Politics and Economics of Competitive Distortions

It is clear that domestic financial services firms can be highly sensitive to competition from foreign-based players in various dimensions of their activities where natural entry barriers are limited. Market penetration threatens to erode returns, and raises the classic set of rent-seeking motivations.

Given the economic interests involved, it can be argued that banks and other financial institutions are in an excellent position to convert these interests into political power. They are often exceedingly well connected politically, and their lobbying capabilities can be awesome indeed. In some cases the financial institutions themselves are government owned and may thus have direct access to the levers of protection. They can form strong coalitions by engaging their clients at both the wholesale and retail levels on their behalf. Moreover, protection in financial services is likely to come through the regulatory process, and to the extent that financial institutions have co-opted the regulators to their mutual benefit, access to the vehicles of protection is facilitated.

In marshalling the arguments, however, financial institutions seeking protection are in some ways on weaker grounds than manufacturing firms. First, they cannot argue convincingly that there will be significant job losses and adjustment costs as a result of market penetration by foreigners, since these will tend to absorb roughly the same number of employees with roughly the same skill content in the same location. Indeed, it is possible that participation by foreign firms could lead to significant employment gains in the domestic financial services sector.

It is also true that a substantial share of financial services is sold to producers of goods and services in the national economy, rather than to ultimate consumers. Shielding from import competition therefore has a high effective protection content and erodes the international competitive performance of other industries. Interests indirectly affected in this manner can be expected to resist protectionism in the financial services sector, alongside consumers whose welfare is directly eroded through credit costs, deposit rates, and the cost and quality of retail financial services.

On the other hand, financial institutions may be able to use the externalities and infant industry arguments in support of their cause. As an integral part of the national payments system, the banking and financial services industry is a source of significant external benefits for society at large. The same is true of its safekeeping function, its role in financial intermediation, and its role as a "transmission belt" for monetary policy. It can thus be argued that financial services represent a "public good," whose private costs and returns do not accurately reflect social costs and returns, therefore justifying protection.

Whether financial institutions are domestically or foreign owned, economists would reply, has nothing to do with any of these issues. Non-discriminatory regulation can assure that financial institutions continue to provide the full range of external benefits in most cases, and in problem cases (e.g., the availability of rural bank branches) targeted government subsidies can take care of maintaining external benefits—perhaps better than cross-subsidization by protected domestic financial institutions. The public-good characteristics of the industry can thus be maintained, while at the same time achieving the static and dynamic gains associated with increased competition.

The infant industry argument, on the other hand, may be more difficult to deal with in a political context. On the one hand, domestic financial institutions are never really "infants" in the classic sense, since all countries have had them since their emergence as nation-states. On the other hand, many financial services are today relatively knowledge- and technology-intensive, with scale and scope economies often giving a decisive competitive edge as well. Hence it is possible, even likely, that domestic financial institutions in many countries are comparatively "retarded," and would indeed have a difficult time competing with outsiders capable of importing know-how at very low marginal cost.

Yet retarded financial sectors can have an adverse impact on the process of economic development by supplying substandard channels of savings into investment, inefficient payments mechanisms and high transactions costs, discouraging economic activity and possibly encouraging capital flight. Competition from foreign-based financial institutions, perhaps in partnership with local interests and using primarily local human resources, can give such institutions a run for their money and create large potential allocative and dynamic gains for the national economy. One critical factor in this respect has been the development of offshore markets, which make it clear to countries how costly distortions can be for the national economy and how lagging liberalization and deregulation can impair both a country's chances of maintaining efficient capital markets *and* its institutions' chances of becoming world-class competitors.

Such arguments notwithstanding, the infant industry case remains a powerful force in the political context, especially when combined with the assertion that inroads by foreign-based institutions would somehow lead to an erosion of national sovereignty.

Incidence of Domestic Regulation

Once having gained entry to a particular market, foreign-based financial institutions generally become fully subject to domestic monetary policy and supervisory and regulatory controls. At this point there are three possibilities: (1) domestic controls, in law or in administrative practice, fall *less seriously* on foreign players than on their domestic competitors; (2) the nominal incidence of regulation is *identical* for both; or (3) foreign players are subjected to *more restrictive* regulation than their local competitors.

The first option seems to be a relatively rare occurrence. Probably the most important case in point involved foreign banks in the United States prior to the passage of the International Banking Act of 1978 (IBA). Foreign-based institutions were exempt from membership in the Federal Reserve System, from the Bank Holding Company Act and the McFadden Act restrictions on branching across state lines, and from the Glass-Steagall prohibitions against an institution's involvement in both commercial and investment banking. The IBA eliminated this discrimination in favor of foreign players, except that institutions already involved in both commercial and investment banking—and those already having branches in multiple states—were grandfathered. This created a degree of tension that has become more important with the continued securitization of financial flows in the United States.

Given the continued restrictive effect of Glass-Steagall in the U.S. domestic market on their U.S. competitors, the 15 foreign banks that were grandfathered under the International Banking Act of 1978 (and could thus maintain both a commercial and investment banking presence in the U.S. market) as well as foreign-based securities houses that are principal competitors to U.S. commercial and investment banks intentionally generally tread softly in exercising their full potential power in the U.S. capital market. In 1986, however, they began to flex their muscles. Nomura Securities and Daiwa Securities led significant issues in the U.S. market for prime names. Sumitomo Bank and Trust Company purchased a 12.5 percent share in Goldman Sachs, in the face of Article 65, Japan's version of Glass-Steagall, albeit under tight restrictions on the part of the Federal Reserve. Securities affiliates of Swiss Bank Corporation, Union Bank of Switzerland, and Deutsche Bank led 15 debt issues amounting to over $2.5 billion during 1986. American commercial banks that were attempting to be major players in global finance saw some of their principal rivals do deals in their own market that were prohibited to them—a rare case of foreign firms being treated significantly more favorably than domestic firms, and being able to exploit that treatment in developing their worldwide competitive positioning.

The Issue of Reciprocity

The Oxford English Dictionary defines reciprocity as "mutual or correspondent concession of advantages or privileges, as forming the basis for the commercial relations between countries." The principle of reciprocity as it is conventionally applied to trade in financial services implies that a country discriminates in its treatment of foreign firms by affording each of them exactly the same treatment the country's own firms receive in its home country. Reciprocity is therefore analogous to retaliation in trade policy. By treating foreign-based firms the same as the foreign government treats home-country firms there, a country may hope to improve the mutual investment climate. One of the arguments in favor of reciprocity in the provision of financial services is that it will maintain overall barriers at a lower level than passive acceptance of unilaterally imposed impediments to open competition.

In the case of trade in goods, reciprocity is certainly easier to define than in services. Swaps of tariff concessions on particular volumes of trade have formed the basis for reciprocity in past trade negotiations. But there is no comparable standard for measuring reciprocity in financial services. Access to a particular market for a particular set of firms may carry entirely different significance from access to another market for another set of players. Understanding reciprocity in this context clearly requires an intimate knowledge of markets, products and competitors.

Nor is it always clear that reciprocity is in the interest of firms seeking access to foreign markets, in whose interests it is ostensibly being applied. Strict reciprocity, for example, would require foreign countries to apply geographic branching limitations and Glass-Steagall–type restrictions to U.S. financial institutions doing business there, which even Japan does not do.

On the other hand, reciprocity is often espoused as the most equitable standard for a foreign presence in the domestic provision of financial services. In practice, however, full reciprocity encounters a number of pitfalls that make it virtually impossible to administer in its narrowest form and very few countries appear to adhere strictly to such a policy, although many include reciprocity in their consideration of other factors related to the entry of foreign banks.

In drafting the International Banking Act of 1978, for example, the U.S. Congress in effect rejected reciprocity in favor of "national treatment," putting foreign-based financial institutions on the same competitive footing as domestic institutions. To apply the concept of reciprocity in its strictest sense would conceivably have required 33 different policies covering foreign banks from the 33 different countries represented in the United States at the time. Such a policy would necessarily have been largely reactive in nature and would have resulted in an incoherent amalgam of petty regulations entirely inconsistent with the objectives of equity and efficiency of the U.S. financial system.

Reciprocity has perhaps been most widely used in recent years with respect to Japan, perhaps in part a reaction to the perceived lack of Japanese reciprocity over the years with respect to trade in industrial goods, and in part a response to the attractiveness of the Japanese capital market as the second largest in the world. It is doubtful that 36 foreign firms would have obtained securities licenses, or that the Tokyo Stock Exchange would have accepted six foreign members in December 1985 without threats of retaliation from the United States, the United Kingdom, and Switzerland. Foreign players have used this opening to good advantage.

In December 1986 the Federal Reserve Bank of New York awarded licenses as primary securities dealers to only two Japanese securities houses, Nomura and Daiwa (instead of all four that applied), and made it clear that even these licenses could be revoked in the absence of significant further progress in opening Japan's securities industry to U.S. firms. A third Japanese firm, the Industrial Bank of Japan, had already gained access to this market by acquiring a U.S. primary government bond dealer, Aubrey Lanston & Co., through its subsidiary, J. Henry Schroder Corp, and Nikko Securities was added later.

The issue of reciprocity came up once again in the context of Japanese direct participation in Wall Street financial houses during 1987, when Nippon Life Insurance bought for $38 million a 13 percent share of Shearson Lehman Brothers from the American Express Company. This followed the 1986 acquisition of shares in Goldman Sachs by Sumitomo Bank. Together with other foreign participations and joint ventures such as Credit Suisse First Boston, the Japanese purchase of Aubrey Lanston & Co., European holdings in Drexel Burnham Lambert, South African holdings in Salomon Brothers, and Arab investments in Smith Barney, the political profile of a strong foreign presence in the U.S. securities industry has grown significantly. The specter was raised of a repeat in the financial services industry of foreign "domination" of the U.S. markets for steel, garments, consumer electronics, and automobiles as foreign (especially Japanese) players developed a strong foothold in U.S. capital markets and acquired world-class training and financial technologies.

This became a fertile ground for raising the issue of reciprocity, and a provision of trade legislation passed by both houses of Congress and vetoed by President Reagan in April 1988 would have required strict reciprocity in major segments of the financial services sector. The focus appeared to be on individual lines of activity, probably reflecting targeted lobbying efforts. For example, while three Japanese securities houses had primary dealer status for government bonds in the United States, no U.S. firms had comparable status in Japan.

A Level Playing Field

Given the structure and motivations underlying distortions of competitive conditions in the financial services industry, "national treatment" would seem to be the substantive equivalent of liberal international trade in this sector. This means that foreign-based players are subject to precisely the same regulatory and prudential controls as domestic players. Yet even this standard can produce differential effects on domestic and foreign-based institutions because of different starting positions and operating characteristics. Further unintended distortions can arise because of stringent home-country capital requirements for institutions doing business in international and foreign markets, where they may compete with players based in other countries who may be treated much more leniently.

Defining a Level Playing Field

What is really required is "equality of competitive opportunity," in the sense of a level playing field—an extraordinarily difficult concept to define, much less to deliver, in the case of an industry as complex as financial services. This can be viewed as comprising the following components:

- Freedom to establish branches, agencies, subsidiaries, representative offices, or other affiliates within a national market on a basis identical to that applying to locally owned financial institutions. In terms of Figure 4.1, freedom of establishment is critical to competitive equality in serving the C- and A-cells within a country, and maximizing the positive linkage effects to cells in the rest of the global matrix. National antitrust and other policies relating to establishment would bear on foreign players identically to domestic players.
- Regulatory symmetry, insofar as possible, with respect to domestic and foreign competitors. This includes the incidence of prudential controls such as capital requirements, asset ratios, lending limits, and reserve requirements. It also involves equality of access to the domestic securities markets, including lead-managing local-currency issues in the local and offshore markets, as well as equal access to the national payments clearing system, money markets and central bank discount facilities, and trust and investment businesses.
- Freedom to import critical resources, including travel and resettlement of professional staff, subscriptions of capital in the case of certain nonbranch affiliates, data processing and telecommunications equipment on the same basis as local firms. Included is equality of access to transborder communication and data transmission.
- Symmetry with respect to the application of exchange controls, if any, as between foreign and local players. This bears on capital outflows such as foreign borrowing in the local markets and local investments abroad, as well as remittances of earnings.
- Equality of access to domestic client groups, financial institutions, and product markets, including branching privileges equal to those of local firms and the right to purchase shares in local financial institutions consistent with domestic laws regarding competition.

Together, these elements provide a consistent set of *benchmarks* for equality of competitive opportunity which, as noted, is the equivalent of liberal trade in the financial services sector. This does not mean that foreign-based financial institutions should be able to avoid the effects of national tax, prudential and monetary control policies, and it is clear that the implementation of a truly level playing field is made vastly more complicated because of these considerations.

New York's Interest in a Level Playing Field

What are the interests of New York as a financial center with respect to the regulatory and market-access context?

First, we have seen that a consistent set of global prudential and regulatory standards, which apply to all "functional" or value-creating financial centers, is fundamentally in the interests of New York. The initiatives taken under the auspices of the Bank for International Settlements over more than a decade, including the risk-based capital standards for banks due to be phased-in by 1983, meet these criteria. The gains from a permanent regulatory uniformity that strikes a tolerable balance between financial soundness and financial efficiency far outweigh what may be disproportionate difficulties that some New York institutions may have in achieving alignment with these standards.

No less desirable is a level playing field relating to the rules governing the competitive micro-structure of the financial markets.

Much of the growth in the New York financial services industry in recent years has been attributable to the expansion of foreign-based banks and securities firms. Not only have they generated substantial employment and other direct and indirect economic benefits, but many have also exhibited greater staying power than local institutions in the presence of adverse market developments. This has probably contributed materially to greater stability in these benefits than might otherwise have prevailed, and has added an important source of stability to the New York economy.

New York has thus benefited significantly from U.S. adherence to "national treatment" with respect to financial services. Only the McFadden Act, the Bank Holding Company Act, and the Glass-Steagall Act remain to favor foreign-based institutions grandfathered under the International Banking Act of 1978, and at the same time continue to burden New York institutions in their efforts to access fully the domestic U.S. markets on a nationwide basis and use it as a viable staging area for competition in global markets.

It is equally important that foreign onshore financial markets be comparably opened-up to U.S. banks and securities firms, most of them based in New York. A good deal of liberalization has already occurred in Canada, Australia, and a few developing countries as well as Europe and Japan. More will be forthcoming in Japan under external and internal pressure, and in Europe in the context of the scheduled 1992 financial market integration in the EEC. Some liberalization can even be expected in developing countries as the efficiency costs of excessive financial regulation and protectionism becomes increasingly apparent—and as they are put under pressure in the Uruguay Round of GATT trade negotiations, which for the first time cover financial services. It is clearly in the interests of New York to achieve a maximum opening of these foreign markets for financial value-added created here—even under threat of possible retaliation in the absence of substantive liberalization.

The difficulty in all of this is that regulatory and market-access policies are made at the national level. Hence it will be up to New York's political representatives to see to it that its interests are fully taken into account in this regard.

Future of New York as a Financial Center

In this chapter, we have documented the tremendous increase in the range of financial products that has developed and the dimensions of the intense competition among financial service firms worldwide. Regulation is a key factor affecting depositor and investor confidence in financial markets and affecting the cost of supplying financial services nationally and globally from a particular financial center. As communications costs decline and capital mobility increases, financial firms can entertain a broader range of locational choices. In this context, how is New York likely to fare in the years ahead?

In the last section we argued that New York's long-term interests would be served by a level playing field regarding regulation. But other factors in addition to regulation help determine which country can claim title as an international financial center and which metropolis becomes its national financial center.

We propose to consider the future of New York as a financial center in two stages: first, will New York continue as the financial capital of the United States, and second, will the United States retain its position as an international financial center? To organize our analysis, we draw on the ten factors cited previously:

- central bank
- culture
- tradition
- economies of scale
- central location
- administrative capital
- transport
- national and local policies
- corporate headquarters
- currency/investment position

The competitive pressures bearing on New York are many. First, financial futures markets, based heavily in Chicago, have grown rapidly in importance. While the New York Stock Exchange and U.S. Treasury securities markets were once the undisputed leaders, with financial futures markets playing the satellite role, there are many who believe that these roles have now been reversed. News affecting market prices is first reflected in financial futures markets and, with a short lag, subsequently reflected in the New York cash markets. In this view, "price discovery" takes place in Chicago. The long-standing tradition of futures trading, scale economies, and centralized location, based on commodities trading, gives Chicago an advantage in financial futures and options.

Second, technological change combined with the high cost of factors of production in New York have given firms an incentive to move "back-office" work out of New York to New Jersey and elsewhere.

Third, technological changes combined with New York taxation and regulation have changed incentives, prompting Citibank to move its credit card operations to South Dakota and other banks to open affiliates in Wilmington, Delaware. Some regulatory and tax changes have been beneficial to New York financial institutions, such as the laws permitting the establishment of International Banking Facilities. New York has also benefited disproportionately from foreign financial institutions expanding into the United States.

Fourth, the loan portfolios and equity values of New York money center banks have been severely hit by LDC debt write-offs, leaving many regional banks in relatively better financial health. This factor, combined with the continuing exodus of major corporations from New York, reduces the importance and influence of a New York operation.

Finally, we note the importance of infrastructure. Financial service firms require a high quality, highly motivated, well-schooled labor force. Environmental problems such as pollution, overcrowding, drugs, crime, and so forth also lessen the appeal of locating in New York. These factors must be viewed in comparison with London, Tokyo, Singapore, Chicago, and elsewhere. As it regards infrastructure, the relative standing of New York City is open to question.

Overall, New York has enjoyed preeminence as the financial center of the United States. Tradition and habit are both strong forces favoring New York to continue in this role. However, changes in the menu of financial products and services, technological change, and other forces are reducing the necessity for financial firms to centralize their activities in New York.

Even if New York were able to retain its role as the financial center of the United States, its prominence would still be affected by the role of the United States within the international financial system. The pattern of economic history has been for the world's largest creditor country to play the leading role in the international financial system. This description fits the British Empire in the nineteenth century and the role of the British Pound and the City of London. It also fits the role played by the United States in shaping the Bretton Woods agreement, the key currency aspect of the U.S. dollar, and the prominence of the New York financial markets.

The distribution of economic and political power today is much more diffuse; the United States is no longer an undisputed, hegemonic power.[18] In absolute terms, the United States has already become the world's largest debtor nation. Japan is the world's largest creditor nation. And the European Community may actually accomplish its goal of internal market harmonization, thrusting it into a more powerful economic position. Most likely, no clear economic hegemony will emerge. The power to shape the international financial system in the future will be shared much more broadly.

Substantial financial wealth has accumulated in the Far East and in Europe. The technology and human capital for establishing efficient financial markets outside of the United States has proven effective. Continuous 24-hour trading is now a reality for some financial instruments and a substantial amount of that trading will occur outside of the United States. As growth rates in Asia and parts of Europe exceed those in the United States, it is likely that financial capital and trading activity will likewise grow at a greater rate outside of the United States.

Regulation set in Washington and elsewhere can affect the balance of financial activity between the United States and the rest of the world. But the United States, as it is no longer a hegemonic power, is unlikely to succeed in assuring that regulation can be slanted to favor the United States. Technological changes in communications and computing also suggest that the costs of decentralized operations have been reduced. These factors taken together suggest that the *relative* prominence of New York as a financial center will decline over the long-run, even if the *absolute* measures of financial activity in New York continue to grow.

Financial services constitute an increasingly mobile industry. New York has in many ways benefited from this mobility in the past, leveraging off its historical role and the availability of economies of scale and scope as a world and national financial center. Nevertheless, the nature of the New York financial services industry makes it disproportionately vulnerable to the next phase in the industry's mobility.

So far, this danger seems to have been largely ignored, swamped by the booming domestic and international financial markets. While the events surrounding October 19, 1987 have raised warning flags, they have led mainly to fiscal belt-tightening designed to ride out hard times on the assumption that there will soon be a return to business as usual. Little serious thought has been given to the underlying competitive parameters that drive New York's performance as a financial center. Even the basic economic analysis is missing—founded on data detailing the aggregate real-sector effects of the financial services industry using regional input-output modeling, for example—and our discussions of this issue with responsible people in the industry several years ago met with profound disinterest. The kind of analysis being done in the United Kingdom on the comparable role of London, or for example in New Jersey on the statewide role of the pharmaceuticals industry, are largely missing here. New York is like the proverbial investment bank that has done superbly well for many years but has neglected to construct the kinds of management and information resources needed for long-term competitive viability.

We would suggest that much greater attention be paid at both the local and state levels to the changes in the financial services industry outlined in this chapter, and their prospective impact on New York. New York must pay much greater attention to its physical and environmental infrastructure and to its human resources. It must carefully reassess its regulatory and taxation systems in the light of those maintained by competitor financial centers. And it must lobby hard for the creation of a rational system of financial regulation at the national level—one that will contribute to a level playing field within which New York based institutions can prosper and one that will continue to attract others to New York.

Notes

1. This section draws heavily on the discussion in Richard M. Levich, "Financial Innovations in International Financial Markets," in M. Feldstein (ed.) *United States in the World Economy* (Chicago: University of Chicago Press, 1988).

2. Informal estimates of the volume of foreign exchange trading in various centers are reported in Group of Thirty, "The Foreign Exchange Market in the 1980s" (New York, 1985), p. 11.

3. Salomon Brothers, Inc., "Prospects for Financial Markets in 1987" (New York), December 1986.

4. Information on swap activity is limited because swaps are carried as off-balance sheet entries and no formal reporting is now required. Estimates by Salomon Brothers and Morgan Guaranty place the volume of interest rate swaps outstanding at the end of 1986 at $300 billion. Currency swaps associated with primary bond issues (so-called swap-driven bond issues) were estimated at $38 billion in 1986, or about 20 percent of new Eurobond issues. Other asset or liability based currency swaps were estimated to be as large as $76 billion. See

Salomon Brothers, "Prospects" (1986) and Morgan Guaranty Trust Co., *World Financial Markets*, December 1986.

5. For an extensive analysis of the effectiveness of Eurodollar futures contracts for hedging dollar interest rate risk and their use as part of a synthetic contract for hedging nondollar interest rate risk, see Annie Koh, *A Study of the Effectiveness of Hedging Dollar and Non-Dollar Borrowing Costs with Eurodollar and Currency Futures*, doctoral dissertation, Graduate School of Business Administration, New York University, 1988.

6. Charles P. Kindleberger, "The Formation of Financial Centers," Princeton Studies in International Finance, No. 36, 1974.

7. Kindleberger, "Formation of Financial Centers," p. 11.

8. Kindleberger, "Formation of Financial Centers," pp. 63–71.

9. Kindleberger, "Formation of Financial Centers," p. 57.

10. Charles P. Kindleberger, *The World in Depression. 1929–1939* (Berkeley: University of California Press, 1973), p. 61.

11. Kindleberger, "Formation of Financial Centers," p. 61.

12. Bank for International Settlements, Annual Report, 1986.

13. The U.S. Treasury's handling of the Netherlands Antilles Treaty in the summer of 1987 could be taken as more recent evidence of official insensitivity toward markets.

14. For a thorough discussion of this issue, see Kenneth W. Dam, *The Rules of the Game* (Chicago: University of Chicago Press, 1982), pp. 320–8. A related problem is that countries may coordinate on a set of financial regulations that are excessively strict or liberal. In this regard, it would be preferable to maintain competition among regulatory authorities. For a complete discussion of this theme, see Edward J. Kane, "Competitive Financial Reregulation: An International Perspective," in R. Portes and A. Swoboda (eds.), *Threats to International Financial Stability* (Cambridge: Cambridge University Press, 1987).

15. Christine Cumming and Laurence Sweet, "Financial Structure of the G-10 Countries: How Does the United States Compare?" *Quarterly Review*, Federal Reserve Bank of New York, 12, No. 4 (Winter 1987–1988): 14–25.

16. For an elaboration on the C-A-P model, see Ingo Walter, *Global Competition in Financial Services* (Cambridge, Mass.: Ballinger–Harper & Row, 1988), Chapter 3.

17. See Organization for Economic Cooperation and Development, *Trade in Services in Banking* (Paris: OECD, 1983); R. M. Pecchioli, *Internationalization of Banking* (Paris: OECD, 1983); U.S. Department of the Treasury, *Report to the Congress on Foreign Government Treatment of U.S. Banking Organizations* (Washington, D.C.: Department of the Treasury, 1979 (updated in 1984)); Ingo Walter, *Barriers to Trade in Banking and Financial Services* (London: Trade Policy Research Centre, 1985); and Sylvia B. Sagari, *The Financial Services Industry: An International Perspective*, doctoral dissertation, Graduate School of Business Administration, New York University, 1986.

18. These themes are developed further by Yoshio Suzuki, "A Prospect for the Future International Monetary System: A Japanese Perspective," New York University, Center for Japan-U.S. Business and Economic Studies, Working Paper No. 53, May 1988.

5

New York's Competitiveness

Thierry Noyelle

In the days that followed Black Monday, gloomy predictions of the securities industry's impending collapse and massive layoffs multiplied, as one forecaster after the other produced even scarier numbers. The implications for New York, it was said, would likely be a sharp and brutal recession in the local economy.

Eight months after the crash, however, events had proven kinder than the doomsayers. Between October 1987 and March 1988 (the latest available government data at the time of this writing), the financial service industries had lost nearly 9,000 jobs, most of which were in the securities industries. Yet, employment in other sectors had grown by an additional 19,000 jobs, leading to a very reasonable 10,000 net job gain in New York City during the six-month period (Table 5.1). Indeed, by the end of the first quarter of 1988, the New York City unemployment rate had dropped to 4.7 percent, its lowest point in 18 years.[1]

New York City forecasters had reason to predict a rapid downturn. Wall Street has a history of large-scale layoffs in the wake of financial crashes. And, of course, there already had been some wrenching adjustments in a number of Wall Street firms, the largest of which came as a result of E.F. Hutton's merger into Shearson Lehman.

Yet banking's radical transformation over the past 15 years would seem to suggest that a different employment scenario is likely to emerge, not simply a repetition of past business cycles. This is so because, as far as corporate and institutional banking is concerned, Wall Street has become Main Street, not simply the place for speculative stock market transactions. Treasury bonds, state and municipal securities, corporate bonds, mortgage-backed securities, junk bonds, commercial paper, and many of the newest instruments introduced in the wake of deregulation have helped to transform Wall Street into a much more diverse and complex marketplace, where a broad range of issuers and investors meet

TABLE 5.1

Employment in New York City Financial Industries, Post–October 1987 Crash (seasonally adjusted)

	October 1987	November 1987	December 1987	January 1988	February 1988	March 1988
SIC 60 Commercial Banking	171,900	172,100	171,900	171,000	171,000	170,100
SIC 62 Securities Industry	159,700	159,300	159,600	157,900	156,600	153,000
SIC 63 Insurance Carriers*	65,200	65,400	65,500	65,500	64,900	65,200
SIC 64 Insurance Agents & Brokers*	29,300	29,500	29,600	30,000	30,100	30,300
SIC 61, 66 & 67 Other Finance	28,300	28,400	28,400	28,500	28,700	28,500
Total Financial Institutions	454,400	454,700	455,000	452,900	451,300	447,100
Total Private Sector Employment	3,021,200	3,021,800	3,025,800	3,034,100	3,034,100	3,031,500

*Not seasonally adjusted; data are from New York State Department of Labor.

Source: U.S. Department of Labor, Bureau of Labor Statistics, New York Regional Office.

to share capital and spread risk and where commercial banks and brokerage houses are often found to compete head-to-head to structure and underwrite deals.

Many of the new markets are unlikely to contract at once in the way in which stock markets historically have contracted during downturns. For example, the federal and trade deficits are unlikely to go away in the near term and Japanese and other foreign investors are likely to continue to need outlets for some of their surpluses. While it is true that new issues of municipal bond markets declined in 1987, following a particularly active market in 1986 in anticipation of tax changes, the market will remain a large and growing one. Also, although the volume of new corporate securities may contract for a while, and while firms may even shift back to old-fashioned bank loans to finance their debt, securitization (the shift from bank to market debt) is unlikely to be reversed.

In short, while some institutions or some markets may fare poorly in the months ahead, others are likely to remain healthy. Indeed, after a period of hesitation in the last quarter of 1987, the corporate bond markets and the market for mergers and acquisitions, leveraged buy-outs, and like financial services have witnessed a new surge of activity since the beginning of the year. And among market participants, there is considerable evidence that while some U.S. firms have retrenched or taken a pause in New York, most foreign firms are still building their local presence.

For example, in an April 1988 article in which *Euromoney* reviewed the market strategy of the big four Japanese securities firms in New York following the crash, the magazine noted that, except for Nomura, which had furloughed some employees in the aftermath of October 19, the other three firms were looking forward to continued employment expansion in New York. The reason: their attempt to venture beyond the U.S. Treasury and cross-border equity markets, where they had established their initial presence, into new markets—mortgage-backed securities, municipal financing, and swaps for Nomura; swaps, mergers and acquisitions, and U.S. domestic equities for Nikko; corporate underwriting for Daiwa; and U.S. domestic equities for Yamaichi.[2] But continued expansion is not limited to the Japanese. A number of European institutions are also busy strengthening their presence in the city (particularly the Italian, French, and German banks) as they see New York as a place in which they cannot afford not to be present in the years ahead.[3]

Of course, this is not to argue that nothing has changed in recent months. Despite the past 15 years of rapid change, international banking is in for more restructuring in the years ahead, as continued high levels of competition and an expected slow-down of growth in a number of markets are likely to weed out some of the weakest participants and transform the matrix of opportunities for all. The issue for New York City is whether such restructuring will favor renewed concentration of activities within the city or, on the contrary, induce dispersion, and, if so, what the City can do about it.

This chapter begins by taking a look at eight structural dimensions that contribute to New York's competitiveness as a major financial center, and at incipient centralization or decentralization tendencies that may strengthen or weaken the city's competitive position. These eight dimensions are: the local agglomeration of demand (i.e., the agglomeration of issuers), the local agglomeration of supply (i.e., the agglomeration of investors), the local agglomeration of financial intermediaries, the local environment of innovation, the local technological environment, the local availability and cost of labor, other local operating costs, and the local agglomeration of supporting business service firms.

Following this discussion, the chapter looks at the policy challenges that ongoing changes are posing. In the last analysis, of course, New York's competitiveness is determined by its ability to create an environment that provides for attractive returns to investors, attractive prices for issuers, and attractive value-added margins for financial intermediaries. From a policy point of view, many of the conditions that affect this equation can be influenced by either or both regulatory and public policies.

In thinking through the policy implications of ongoing changes, City and State officials must be able to recognize where and when the city's interests lie above and beyond that of locally based U.S. firms. From New York City's point of view, it does not necessarily matter whether investors, issuers, or intermediaries are domestic or foreign, as long as they help to develop the local market, create new local jobs, and pay local taxes. In this respect, in a world of global markets, New York must take some of its cues from London or Hong Kong whose recent growth stems largely from their respective successes in enticing foreigners to come and conduct business locally.

The distinction between regulatory and public policies is, of course, somewhat arbitrary. However, to the extent that the previous chapter by Levich and Walter emphasizes mainly policy issues that fall within the scope of control of the regulators, this one focuses principally on what local and state economic development officials may do to alter and promote the local environment.

Eight Dimensions of Competitiveness

Two major trends have marked the transformation of banking in recent years: globalization and securitization. In its simplest definition, globalization means that suppliers and demanders of capital no longer need to be in the same place to strike deals.[4] Globalization is a process that was made possible by deregulation, including the lifting of restrictions on capital movement, but rendered necessary since the mid-1970s by the need to recycle large financial surpluses linked to large trade imbalances, involving first the OPEC countries and, lately, Japan.

Securitization refers to the trend toward channelling a greater share of financial assets through marketable securities rather than through old-fashioned bank debt.[5] It is also a process that has been facilitated by deregulation, but one that finds its origins partly in the inflation of the late 1970s and early 1980s. By widening margins between return paid to depositors or interest paid by borrowers and the yield received by commercial banks, inflation encouraged borrowers and depositors to find new and more competitive means to satisfy their needs. These were found in the money and security markets.

Based on the past ten years, one might argue that globalization has tended to weaken the role of New York as a financial center by undermining its earlier oligopolistic power: witness the formidable expansion of the London-based Euromarkets during the mid-1980s. By comparison, securitization, by strengthening the role of market forces, could probably be shown to have benefited large financial centers such as New York, or even London and Tokyo, because it requires an agglomeration of issuers, investors, and market-makers to promote better circulation of information on which market mechanisms thrive. The outcome might best be described as a simultaneous process of decentralization and concentration: decentralization in the sense that New York no longer holds the overwhelming financial-size advantage that it once held; but concentration in the sense that wholesale/investment financial activity once relatively diffused throughout a worldwide network of money and regional banking centers has become increasingly concentrated in a few key markets: New York, London, Tokyo, Hong Kong, Singapore, Frankfurt, and a few others. The intriguing question for the future is whether the same trends can be expected to continue or, on the contrary, to unravel. The following paragraphs take a look at some of the forces that may affect the current equilibrium.

The Agglomeration of Demand

A preliminary observation is that the trend toward securitization will continue for the very same reasons that it occurred in the first place. By making for a more competitive environment, securitization allows for more favorable pricing for issuers. In addition, securitization allows for a more extensive distribution of risks among investors and financial intermediaries, with the continuing depressing impact of Third World and Latin American debts on the balance sheets of commercial banks around the world serving as a powerful reminder of the costs of concentrated risks. So, even though the past few months may have seen a partial shift back to traditional bank loans, an extensive reversal of the trend seems quite unlikely in the medium and long run.

As the trend progresses, new issuers are likely to be drawn in. They may be large corporate and institutional customers from countries where the trend toward securitization is less advanced; they may also be smaller-sized customers, thus far too small to have entered the securities markets. This may have several implications for New York's capital markets.

New York remains the economic center of a $4.5 trillion economy, twice larger than its nearest rival, Japan. While size alone may ensure that New York will remain a large center for new issues, the fact that securitization is more advanced in the United States than elsewhere may also mean that growth will be slower, unless it attracts a disproportionate share of new issuers from abroad.

In general, concentration of expertise among New York-based financial institutions should ensure continued high levels of new issue activities, especially in product areas where competition is only weakly price-sensitive, and is, instead, strongly influenced by the issuers' needs for financial expertise or even proximity to certain investors. In this respect, as more foreign firms seek to develop a market for their shares among U.S. investors, New York should be able to be able to develop a strong market for ADRs (American Deposit Rights).[6]

On the other hand, in those areas of banking where services have become increasingly standardized and commodified and where issuers are most price sensitive, globalization will likely continue to drive demand toward the lowest cost centers. In part, this is what explains the rise of London in the mid-1980s. A high dollar and a much looser regulatory environment in the offshore London market made for markedly lower pricing of new issues in that city. Between 1980 and 1986, new Eurobond issues in London grew from approximately $50 to $190 billion, while U.S. domestic corporate bond issues grew from $100 to $230 billion and Japanese domestic issues from $17 to $65 billion.[7]

In the years ahead, however, such a market logic may favor New York or Tokyo over London. In just a few years, the rapid drop in the value of the dollar has turned New York from one of the most expensive financial centers to operate in, into one of the cheapest. In addition, partly as a result of its own success and partly as a result of recent attempts by central bankers from key advanced economies to jointly regulate markets, London may be losing its earlier regulatory advantage.[8]

Finally, Japanese issuers, who in the mid-1980s had looked to London as a favored location to raise straight and convertible debt, may be drawn back to Tokyo as it deregulates. Indeed, in the early months of 1988, there were indications of a shift in new issue activity away from London.

Lastly, to the extent that the trend toward securitization continues, it may also imply trying to bring to the securities markets firms or institutions which, at present, remain outside their reach because of size, provided that the information support infrastructure provided by the rating and financial information firms can keep pace with the demand. Here too, the implications for New York may be mixed.

New entrants in the securities markets demand a much greater level of support and expertise from financial intermediaries in structuring issues. This should favor the large New York institutions where expertise is often more developed than elsewhere. But if large numbers of such new entrants are likely to come from among the nation's pool of middle-market firms, then New York–based institutions may be at a disadvantage since, traditionally, they have not been well connected to this class of customers.

Table 5.2 shows the lead managers for initial public offerings (IPOs) in 1986 and the first half of 1987. The table suggests a strong role for second-tier and regional security firms as witnessed by the rankings of Wheat Securities and Alex Brown & Sons, respectively number two and three, as well as the showing of other small firms among the top 25. One banker interviewed for this study went as far as suggesting that, with reform of the Glass-Steagall Act looming, the regional banks, by virtue of their long-standing relationship to the corporate middle-market firms, could present a major source of new competition if they tried to use their new powers to bring such customers to the securities markets.

The Agglomeration of Supply

Another source of New York's competitive strength is the city's position at the center of the world's largest pool of institutional investment funds.

Table 5.3, based on data gathered by InterSec for *Euromoney*, shows the location of the largest pools of institutional funds, ranked by the cumulated assets of the 130 largest institutional investors worldwide (this group comprises all institutional investment funds with a value of more than $13 billion in 1986, including pension funds, mutual funds, and funds managed by banks and insurance companies). In 1986, U.S. institutional investors controlled roughly 60 percent of those largest funds worldwide, four times as much as their nearest rival, the Japanese

TABLE 5.2
Initial Public Offerings, 1986, 1987

1987 Rank	1986 Rank		First Half 1987		1986	
			Amount $ million	Share %	Amount $ million	Share %
1	1	Merrill Lynch	1,999	13.88	2,410	10.95
2	16	Wheat First Securities	1,950	13.54	358	1.63
3	14	Alex Brown & Sons	1,843	12.79	516	2.35
4	3	Goldman Sachs	1,812	12.62	1,652	7.51
5	5	Shearson Lehman	1,197	8.31	1,434	6.51
6	2	Drexel Burnham	586	4.07	1,975	8.97
7	—	Wertheim Schroeder	497	3.45	—	—
8	12	Kidder Peabody	413	2.87	648	2.9
9	6	First Boston	409	2.84	1,342	6.0
10	68	Morgan Keegan	274	1.90	14	0.0
. . . .						
13	44	Oppenheimer	232	1.62	39	0.1
. . . .						
20	25	Robinson-Humphrey	103	0.71	118	0.5
21	—	Edward D. Jones	93	0.65	—	—
. . . .						
23	35	Hambrecht & Quist	77	0.54	50	0.2
24	28	Ladenburg Thalmann	77	0.54	78	0.3
25	26	Robertson, Colman, Stephens	73	0.51	90	0.4

Source: *Euromoney*, September 1987.

institutional investors. The greater New York area alone was the seat to nearly half of the U.S. total.

While contributing to the strength of New York as a financial center, it is true that large concentrations of funds do not guarantee that investment managers will operate in the local market. Indeed, Swiss institutional investors (dominated by the large Swiss banks), which, according to Table 5.3, control the third largest country pool, invest mostly in the Euromarkets, with a good deal of investment management activity taking place in London. I will return to this point in the policy section.

The Agglomeration
of Financial Intermediaries

Tables 5.4 and 5.5 present two sets of rankings: a list of the 20 largest U.S. banking centers ranked by the cumulated assets of the nation's top 100 bank holding companies and three lists of the world's 12 largest banking centers ranked respectively by the cumulated net income, cu-

TABLE 5.3
Location of 130 Largest Institutional Investors Worldwide,[1] Cumulated Assets by Country and Major Metro Area (U.S. Only), 1986

	$ billions		Share %
United States	2,597.6		60.0
Greater New York	1,190.9		27.5
New York		911.1	
Newark, N.J.		145.1	
Trenton-Princeton, N.J.		102.1	
Fairfield, Ct.		32.6	
Boston	342.5		7.9
Hartford	186.2		4.3
Chicago	133.2		3.0
San Francisco	106.8		2.5
Los Angeles	90.1		2.1
Philadelphia	72.8		1.7
Sacramento	58.6		1.4
Albany	46.6		1.1
Columbus	44.4		1.0
Other metro centers	325.5		
Japan	640.0		14.8
Switzerland	540.0		12.5
United Kingdom	252.7		5.8
Netherlands	90.2		2.1
West Germany	64.5		1.5
Other Countries	145.3		
Total	4,330.3		100.0

[1]$13 billion of assets under management or more in 1986.

Source: InterSec data in *Euromoney*, September 1987.

mulated assets, and the average net income to asset ratios of the world's top 50 commercial banks and top 25 investment banks. The results are by now familiar.

Table 5.4, which compares 1979 and 1986, shows the decline of the nation's other money centers—San Francisco and Chicago—relative to New York, the buildup of Los Angeles' strength and the emergence of new regional banking centers that derive their strength from the presence of commercial banking institutions specialized in highly profitable consumer and corporate middle markets. In fairness to Chicago, by its very nature, this ranking overlooks that city's growing importance in the new capital markets through its options and futures exchanges.[9]

TABLE 5.4
Twenty Largest U.S. Banking Cities Ranked by the Cumulated Assets of the Top 100 Bank Holding Corporations, 1979, 1986

1986 rank	6/30/86 $ billions assets	# firms	%	1979 rank	12/31/79 $ billions assets	%	Change in rank + or (−)
1 New York	611,701	12	33.75	1	362,671	36.16	0
2 San Francisco	166,279	3	9.17	2	145,120	14.37	0
3 Los Angeles	112,134	3	6.19	4	54,610	5.44	+1
4 Chicago	85,912	4	4.74	3	78,435	7.82	−1
5 Boston	71,411	5	3.94	6	24,659	2.46	+1
6 Dallas	69,532	4	3.84	5	28,673	2.86	−1
7 Pittsburgh	56,311	2	3.11	11	21,730	2.17	+4
8 Minn.-St. Paul	46,935	2	2.59	9	24,569	2.45	+1
9 Charlotte	43,242	2	2.39	16	9,485	0.95	+7
10 Houston	43,066	3	2.38	8	24,581	2.45	−2
11 Detroit	42,673	4	2.35	10	24,496	2.44	−1
12 Atlanta	36,264	2	2.00	20	5,855	0.58	+8
13 Philadelphia	31,527	4	1.74	7	24,586	2.45	−6
14 Cleveland	30,103	3	1.66	12	16,447	1.64	−2
15 Newark	24,925	2	1.38	17	8,330	0.83	−2
16 Buffalo	24,532	1	1.35	13	15,728	1.57	−3
17 Jacksonville	22,537	2	1.24	21	5,798	0.58	+4
18 St. Louis	20,527	3	1.13	18	8,137	0.81	0
19 Columbus	18,235	2	1.01	15	10,081	1.01	−4
20 Albany	17,779	2	0.98	31	3,963	0.40	+11
			86.92%			89.13%	
Top 100	1,812,682	100	100.00%		1,003,044	100.00%	

Source: "The 100 Largest Bank Holding Companies," *American Banker*, September 30, 1986, and "The 100 Largest Bank Holding Companies," *Moody's Finance Manuals*, 1980.

TABLE 5.5
Top Twelve Banking Centers Ranked by Cumulated Net Income, Cumulated Assets, and Average Net Income to Asset Ratio of the Top 50 Commercial Banks and Top 25 Securities Firms, 1985, 1986

A. Ranked by Income ($ millions)

1986 Rank	1985 Rank	Cities	1986 Income	1986 # Firms	1985 Income	1985 # Firms
1	2	Tokyo	6424	22	2922	20
2	1	New York	5673	16	5372	14
3	3	London	2934	5	2282	10
4	4	Paris	1712	6	983	6
5	8	Osaka	1261	4	617	4
6	6	Frankfurt	1003	3	763	3
7	11	Zurich	826	2	337	1
8	14	Amsterdam	739	3	172	1
9	13	Basel	415	1	291	1
10	10	Hong Kong	392	1	348	1
11	7	Los Angeles	386	1	636	2
12	9	Montreal	354	1	605	2

B. Ranked by Assets ($ billions)

1986 Rank	1985 Rank	Cities	1986 Assets	1985 Assets
1	1	Tokyo	1801.4	1086.3
2	2	New York	904.8	846.0
3	3	Paris	659.3	543.7
4	5	Osaka	557.6	366.7
5	4	London	390.3	376.3
6	6	Frankfurt	306.8	228.8
7	13	Amsterdam	193.4	51.4
8	17	Munich	133.4	53.7
9	10	Nagoya	123.9	77.7
10	8	San Francisco	109.2	118.5
11	15	Kobe	107.1	61.2
12	11	Hong Kong	90.8	68.8

C. Ranked by Net Income to Asset Ratio (%)

1986 Rank	1985 Rank	Cities	1986 Ratio	1985 Ratio
1	3	London	0.752	0.606
2	1	New York	0.627	0.636
3	2	Los Angeles	0.617	0.621
4	4	Toronto	0.591	0.527
5	6	Zurich	0.524	0.502
6	6	Montreal	0.520	0.502
7	8	Basel	0.489	0.475
8	5	Hong Kong	0.432	0.506
9	9	Amsterdam	0.382	0.333
10	11	Tokyo	0.357	0.269
11	10	Frankfurt	0.327	0.330
12	12	Paris	0.260	0.170

Source: "Global Finance and Investment," Special Report, Worldscope, *Wall Street Journal*, September 29, 1986, and September 18, 1987.

Table 5.5, which compares 1985 and 1986, underlines the rise of Tokyo as a headquarter location for the world's largest financial institutions when measured by assets. When measured in income terms, however, the findings are somewhat different. While by 1986 Tokyo stood at the top of the ranking by cumulated net income, the ranking based on net income to asset ratios favored U.S., U.K., Canadian, and Swiss head-quartered institutions over the Japanese, suggesting that as a group, Japanese institutions had been slower at effecting the shift from asset-driven growth to profit-driven growth, implicit in part in the trend toward securitization. This may be changing, however.

As the *Euromoney* article cited above noted,[10] the era of Japanese banking expansion based on market-share growth at razor-thin margins may be ending, in the aftermath of the Japanese investment firms' debacle in the Eurobond markets in the summer of 1987 and as Japanese commercial banks find themselves under pressure to build up their capital base to meet the new capital requirements agreed upon by the Group of 12 under the auspices of the Bank for International Settlements last fall.[11] While how this might affect those rankings is unclear, clearly the Japanese institutions will remain formidable competitors in the years ahead.

The implications for New York need not be bad however. As was noted earlier, foreign banking presence in New York—Japanese or otherwise—is still growing. This is in contrast to London, where recent months have seen mostly retrenchment by foreign banks. In other words, the agglomeration of financial intermediaries in New York is still gaining strength, not weakening.

The Environment of Innovation

A fourth dimension of New York's competitiveness is financial in-novation. More rapid innovation is in part a reflection of the shortening of the product cycle, itself a function of the intensification of competition. By starting the trend toward financial deregulation, which over the years contributed to the intensification of competition, U.S. regulators helped to establish New York as the leading center for financial innovation.[12] But financial innovation can be fast fleeting. It can easily be reproduced elsewhere. And whatever advantage New York-based institutions may gain elsewhere from being on the front line of innovation in New York may not last long.

For example, Table 5.6 shows the leading dealers in Euro-commercial paper in 1986 and during the first half of 1987. Within a year, the U.S. banks, which ranked at the top of the market as it came into life, saw themselves dislodged, mostly by British firms. Indeed, Merrill Lynch,

TABLE 5.6
Euro-commercial Paper Dealers, 1986, 1987

1987 Rank	1986 Rank		First Half of 1987		1986	
			No. of Issues	Amount $ million	No. of Issues	Amount $ million
1	3	Swiss Bank Corp.	36	8,362	58	18,206
2	14	County Natwest Ltd.	33	6,055	22	3,996
3	4	SG Warburg & Co.	32	7,179	58	14,181
4	1	Citicorp Investment Bank	30	6,172	77	18,059
5	9	Chase Investment Bank	22	5,926	28	6,005
6	5	Morgan Guaranty Ltd.	19	3,861	58	13,994
7	7	Morgan Guaranty Intl.	18	6,639	49	19,530
8	19	Morgan Greenfell	18	4,020	14	2,866
9	17	Barclays Bank Corp.	18	3,484	17	3,512
10	8	Shearson Lehman	17	6,321	41	16,705

Source: *Euromoney*, 1987.

ranked number 2 in 1986, did not even rank in the top 10 during the first half of 1987.

Another example is swaps. While at the end of 1986 U.S. commercial and investment banks still ranked at the top of the list, there were indications that firms from other countries were quickly moving up the rankings, partly because innovation had diffused rapidly and partly because they were able to use their own particular strengths to their own advantages (Table 5.7). As one observer noted recently, "As swaps expand, they involve an increasingly larger number of currencies and make for more and more volatile deals. In U.S. dollars, everyone has access to U.S. treasuries and information about how to hedge. With currencies such as Australian dollars, D-marks, ECU or Sterling, you must be in the domestic market."[13] This, according to the same observer, helped explain the recent rise of firms such as Natwest, Deutsche Bank, and Banque Paribas.

Nevertheless, New York continues to innovate, witness, for example, the range of financial engineering developed in recent years around the booming markets for mergers and acquisitions (M&A), leveraged buyouts (LBOs), and other asset restructuring deals. Here, however, two trends may transform the dynamics of this relatively new market in the years ahead.

To the extent that M&A business becomes increasingly tied to cross-border transactions in conjunction with the rise of foreign direct investment in the United States, then there is an opportunity for non-New York-based institutions to learn the expertise and to partially transfer out of New York activity which earlier would have taken place

TABLE 5.7
Leading Firms in Swaps, 1986

		Volume of Outstanding Swaps ($ billions)
1	Citibank	30–45
	Bankers Trust	30–45
	Salomon Brothers	30–45
4	Morgan Guaranty	15–25
	Chase Manhattan	15–25
	Chemical Bank	15–25
	First Chicago	15–25
	Prudential Bache	15–25
9	First Boston	13–15
	Bank America	13–15
	Security Pacific	13–15
	Kleinwort Benson	13–15
12	Shearson-Lehman	10–12
	Manufacturers Hanover	10–12
	Merrill Lynch	10–12
	Banque Paribas	10–12
	Union Bank of Switzerland	10–12
	Nomura	10–12
18	Swiss Bank Corp.	4–10
	Lloyds	4–10
	First Interstate	4–10
	Morgan Stanley	4–10
	Deutsche Bank	4–10
	Morgan Greenfell	4–10
	Drexel Burnham Lambert	4–10

Source: *Euromoney*, September 1987.

exclusively here. This is shown by the changes in the rankings of the leading advisers for international M&A between 1986 and 1987 shown in Table 5.8. By 1987, five new U.K. merchant banks had joined the two already present in 1986 among the top 13 advisers. Also, as M&A activity develops in Europe—and there are signs to this effect—there will be plenty of opportunities for expertise to develop abroad.[14]

A second trend transforming the market is the emergence of the boutique investment firms. Table 5.9 shows that the boutique phenomenon has some real grounding and may even be gaining in strength. The table is based on an analysis of *Fortune* magazine's top 50 deals of the year for 1985, 1986, and 1987. As tabulated by *Fortune*, these deals include the year's largest M&As, LBOs, IPOs, and other securities

TABLE 5.8
Leading Advisors in International Mergers and Acquisitions, 1986, 1987

1987 Rank		Jan 87–Dec 87		Jan 86–June 86		1986 Rank
		$ million	# deals	$ million	# deals	
1	First Boston/CSFB	27,400	72	5,440	20	2
2	Morgan Stanley	9,088	29	7,442	17	1
3	Burns & Fry	6,949	16			not in top 10
4	Merrill Lynch	5,556	20	1,736	16	6
5	Schroder Group	5,293	28			not in top 10
6	Drexel Burnham	5,281	28	2,041	5	4
7	S G Warburg	4,253	21			not in top 10
8	Dillon Read	4,139	9			not in top 10
9	Samuel Montagu	4,111	17	1,090	2	7
10	Shearson Lehman	3,637	23			not in top 10
11	County NatWest	2,834	9			not in top 10
12	Lazard	2,288[1]	23	2,084[2]	11	3
13	Morgan Greenfell	2,056[3]	31	1,931	17	5

[1]London only; excluding NY and Paris.
[2]NY and London, excluding Paris.
[3]London office only.

Source: *Euromoney*, September 1987 and September 1986.

offerings. Among the boutiques, I have included specialist firms such as Kohlberg, Kravis and Roberts, regional securities firms such as Alex Brown & Sons, venture capital firms, and other financial intermediaries not belonging to the group of Wall Street powerhouses. The data show that while the share of "boutique" advisors involved in the top 50 deals grew from roughly 8.5 to 10 percent in 1985 and 1987, their share of fees grew much faster and at levels well above that of the number of deals they had arranged: from 8.1 percent of all fees in 1985 to 27 percent of all fees in 1987. This does confirm the notion that where cutting-edge expertise is what is demanded, scale need not enhance competitiveness. The rise of the "boutique" should work in favor of New York because such a "disintegrated" M&A industry can only work successfully in an environment where strong agglomeration economies are at work. The smaller the firm, the more it depends on the expertise of others (other banks, lawyers, accountants, etc.) and the information that circulates in the marketplace (more on this below).

The Technological Environment

As is the case for innovation, New York is usually regarded as the leading developer of new computerized technology in the financial services. Indeed, the two are largely linked since financial innovation is increasingly based in part on the development of new computer-

TABLE 5.9
Top Fifty Deals of the Year, 1985–1987

| | 1987 | | | | 1986 | | | | 1985 | | | |
	# Advisors	%	Fees $ millions	%	# Advisors	%	Fees $ millions	%	# Advisors	%	Fees $ millions	%
"Boutiques"[1][2]	12	10.2	312.4	27.0	11	10.0	169.1	16.4	8	8.5	47.1	8.1
All firms	118	100.0	1,157.0[3]	100.0	110	100.0	1,033.3[4]	100.0	94	100.0	582.1[5]	100.0

[1]As defined by *Fortune* magazine. Includes the largest M&A, LBOs, IPOs, and other securities offerings.
[2]See text for definition.
[3]Fees are not available for 34 of the 118 positions.
[4]Fees are not available for 12 of the 110 positions.
[5]Fees are not available for 11 of the 94 positions.

Source: *Fortune*, February 1, 1988; February 2, 1987; January 20, 1986.

driven products and processes. To return to the example of swaps, it is in part the expertise of New York-based institutions in developing computer systems that explains their lead. "A good risk-monitoring system is crucial and requires a huge investment in time and capital. For that reason, the swap game is open only to those players that have made a major commitment" notes a banker from Chase Manhattan.[15]

Likewise, New York-based institutions have been at the cutting-edge of the introduction of new trading techniques in the stocks, futures, and options markets heavily dependent on sophisticated computer systems.[16]

But the introduction of new technology has often been a two-sided development, in that it has both helped to protect the competitive edge of New York-based institutions and made it possible to reorganize activities away from the city. First, the introduction of new technology has helped to rationalize back-office work, but such rationalization has often been accompanied by a search for locations characterized by lower clerical costs. In other words, on-line processing technology has accelerated the move of back-office work outside the city at the same time that it has helped firms to improve their cost competitiveness.

Second, the introduction of new technology is contributing to a major transformation of front-office work, especially in trading areas. By making market information increasingly ubiquitous, screen-based technology is making trading increasingly less dependent on the need for a central market location and undermining the monopoly of traders and brokers over market information. The result is a loosening of the ties between traders and the city and growing pressure to eliminate intermediation by dealers and brokers. A banker interviewed for this study noted that one government security broker, Kantor Fitzgerald, had already installed trading screens with institutional investors.

The Availability and Cost of Labor

New York is recognized to have a major competitive advantage in terms of high-level human resources. In part, this is a product of the fact that the U.S. economy produces more college-educated individuals than any other country, including at the graduate school level where the country has a major lead. It is also a product of local area schools, such as New York University and a few others that have played a major role in offering training and retraining opportunities for executives, managers, and professionals employed by the financial industries.

Equally as important, however, may be the fact that the labor market for financial specialists and managers has changed the fastest and the furthest in New York. To a large degree, the transformation of financial markets has been based on an extensive diversification of the product range, and diversification has meant specialization. As noted in a recent study by the OECD, an open labor market system that allows specialists to change jobs frequently is one of the important ways in which human resource expertise can be built.[17] New York has been at the vanguard of the transformation toward more open labor markets in the financial sector.

The downside of this open labor market system for skilled professionals and managers is often perceived as over-inflated salaries. But competition seems to be partially taking care of the problem. Indeed the largest impact of the recent shakeout in the financial sector may have been as much in terms of salary cuts as in terms of job cuts.

After years of go-go expansion, a number of the large investment houses finally priced themselves out of the market, as competition from other institutions, especially the Japanese securities firms and some of the domestic commercial banks, intensified. This was one of the basic reasons for Salomon's dramatic decision to close its entire municipal bond department and to retrench in commercial paper in early October, a move that followed similar but less publicized ones by other firms throughout the summer. In the wake of these early layoffs, there is evidence that many of the newly unemployed found jobs elsewhere, but at a sharp salary discount. Indeed, the New York Regional Office of the Bureau of Labor Statistics estimates that, once adjusted for changes in employment levels, wages and salaries in the financial sector in the Northeast declined approximately 3 percent in the first quarter of 1988, the first time a decline had been registered in many consecutive quarters.[18] In addition, when compared to wage and salary levels in other international financial centers, the sharp drop in the value of the dollar has likely brought New York salaries to much more competitive levels than they might have been earlier in the 1980s.

Whereas New York may have an advantage in terms of skilled personnel, it is probably weaker than it ought to be in terms of its clerical and other middle-level labor force. This problem is not new; it is not unique to the financial industries, and probably not unique to New York. In addition, it is a problem that is unlikely to be solved rapidly. But it is one that must be of concern to the city, short of which pressures to move certain operations out of the city will continue to intensify.

Other Operating Costs

New York faces a major housing crisis and rising congestion costs, the latter being in part a product of the city's own economic success in recent years. While it is true that, relative to Tokyo, New York's housing and congestion problems may seem benign, relative to other U.S. cities they may not, thereby intensifying the pressure for some activities to move out of the city.

Utility costs in New York are also high especially relative to those in its surrounding areas. This is important if one considers that utility costs for a square foot of office space with large computer equipment are almost as high as the underlying rent itself: for example, up to $12–$14 electric costs per square foot compared to $15–$30 rent cost on an annual basis for the New York Penn Plaza midtown area. (The annual electric bill for office space without computers is approximately $2–$3 per square foot.)[19]

The Agglomeration of Support Business Services

Often overlooked but perhaps one of the city's greatest assets, is the local agglomeration of business support services: accounting, legal services, management consulting, data processing, software, advertising, specialized printing and publishing, and so forth. Indeed, the more specialized and complex financial markets become and the more specialization tends to drive vertical or horizontal "disintegration" of the industry (i.e., to fuel the emergence of many specialists firms), the more financial activity becomes dependent on business support firms and on spatial concentration.

Table 5.10 shows a remarkable parallelism in the growth of employment in the city's financial service industries and business support services since 1979. Between 1979 and 1987, employment in financial services grew by an additional 105,000 jobs and employment in business services by 102,000 jobs, each providing nearly a third of a total net new growth of 306,000 jobs.

The expertise of New York-based business services has no equal but perhaps that of London-based firms.[20] Even in some areas of expertise, the London firms are probably one step behind those of New York. For example, as they prepared for Big Bang, London financial institutions called extensively upon the services of New York-based information technology specialists (mostly the management consulting divisions of the Big Eight accounting firms and independent software firms) to develop new systems.[21] Or, in the recent battle over the control of Societe Generale de Belgique, U.S. law firms were called in to figure out legal strategies and implications.[22]

In addition, in light of Tokyo's relatively weaker business service expertise—in part a product of Japan's past protectionism against the entry of foreign business service firms—New York's strength in this area may provide the city with a relatively lasting competitive advantage.

TABLE 5.10
Employment in Financial and Business Services in New York City, 1979, 1987

	1979	1987
SIC 60 Commercial Banking	144,000	172,000
SIC 62 Securities Industry	76,100	156,600
SIC 63 Insurance Carriers	75,700	65,100
SIC 64 Insurance Agents and Brokers	26,400	29,100
SIC 61, 66, 67 Savings & Loan and Other Financial Sectors	23,400	28,100
SIC 73 Business Services (Advertising, Consulting, Software, Others)	228,800	298,000
SIC 81 Legal Services	42,900	68,900
SIC 89 Accounting, Architecture, Engineering	57,000	63,700
Total Finance	345,600	450,900
Total Business, Legal and Accounting Services	328,700	430,600
Total Non-Agricultural Employment	3,278,800	3,584,900
Net increase in Finance 1979–1987	105,300 (34.4%)	
Net increase in Business and Other Services 1979–1987	101,900 (33.3%)	
Net increase in all sectors 1979–1987	306,100 (100.0%)	

Source: U.S. Department of Labor, Bureau of Labor Statistics, New York Regional Office.

Policy Challenges and Opportunities

The volume of financial activity carried out in New York in the years ahead will be determined, in large part, by economic growth within the U.S. and by the capacity of the city to attract new business from within the nation or from abroad. The shrinking size of the United States economy relative to others as well as the growing sophistication of other international financial centers around the world suggest that, in relative terms, New York will continue to decline as center of finance, even though the volume of business should continue to grow. This, of course, is well beyond the influence of local and state public officials.

In addition to continuing to serve its traditional customers, New York's best opportunities for new growth lie in two areas: fostering the internationalization of its markets and bringing new U.S.-based customers to the securities markets. In internationalizing its markets, some observers feel that New York should build on its advantage as the most efficient clearing center. For example, the industry should be encouraged to review what needs to be done to prepare the Depository Trust Corporation for

TABLE 5.11
Foreign Investment as a Percentage of Private Sector Pension Assets, 1980, 1985, 1990

	1980	1985	1990
United States	1	3	8
Japan	1	8	20
U.K.	9	18	25
Germany	2	3	6
France	1	2	4
Canada	7	8	10
Netherlands	4	9	15
Switzerland	4	4	8
Belgium	25	30	35
Australia	0	5	12

Source: "Investment Management Survey," *The Economist*, November 8, 1986, p. 12.

the 1990s. This may involve new, large-scale investments in computerized clearing systems. Also, New York may need to recapture some of the momentum that its equity markets lost as trading activity shifted to Chicago futures and options markets. Current attempts to strengthen linkages between New York and Chicago's markets as well as the NYSE's plans to introduce "basket" contracts should help.[23]

In terms of bringing new U.S. firms to the market, New York suffers from the fact that, historically, New York-based institutions have had a weak relationship with corporate middle-market customers, which, nowadays represent the fastest growing segment of the economy. This is a problem in more than one way and I return to the issue further below. Short of turning New York investment and commercial banks into what they are not, New York officials might want to review what they might do to make it attractive for regional institutions better connected to middle-market customers to bring some of their business to the city. New York's well-developed information systems, powerful clearing mechanisms, and high market liquidity may be part of the pitch.

Even though technology facilitates the movement of capital from one market to the other, New York must make sure that the city and the state remain attractive locations for money and investment managers. Foreign investment, as a percentage of investment assets, remains low among U.S. institutional portfolios when compared to those of foreign investors (see Table 5.11 for a comparison of foreign investment as a percentage of private sector pension assets in ten countries). If foreign markets offer better returns than U.S. ones, then New York, at a minimum, must make sure that New York-based investment managers are not at a competitive disadvantage with those from other states. In particular, as indicated by the InterSec data referred to in Table 5.3, insurance firms are among some of the largest institutional investors in the New York area.[24] Allowing for larger shares of foreign investment by New York insurers may require some intervention on the part of the New York State Insurance Department.

In addition, to keep New York competitive with other states as a place to manage investment may necessitate some reform of City and State corporate income taxes. The issue arose recently, when Dreyfus, one of the largest New-York based mutual fund managers, considered moving its operation to New Jersey, partly to benefit from lower corporate taxes. (Of course, this was not the only reason why Dreyfus contemplated a move; labor force availability and rent differentials were also part of the firm's calculation.) The City and the State promised Dreyfus to act on the issue rapidly, and legislation is now being drafted that would permit mutual funds to apportion management fees and receipts partly on the basis of the location of their shareholders, resulting in a lowering of their corporate tax rate.

Even though technology may in part undermine the attractiveness of the city by facilitating decentralization, New York cannot afford not to stay at the cutting edge of technological developments. Until recently, major telecommunication equipment such as PBXs was counted as part of real estate property, thus increasing the assessed value of real estate for local tax purposes. In essence, the rule acted as a deterrent to new investment. Most likely, this rule ought to be phased out.

The advent of screen-based trading assumes an infrastructure of ever-more powerful computer processing and clearing systems. Historically, banks, financial information companies, and clearing houses have developed systems on their own strength. As some clearing and processing systems continue to increase in size and as development costs increase, the industry may want to take a look to determine where systems serve a "public utility" function and might best be developed jointly. The State might be able to help by involving the New York State Technology and Science Foundation, which, in turn, could involve university-based computer scientists in R&D efforts.

The State and the City have room to intervene and tilt some of the technological trends in New York's favor in some other ways. First, the City has had some success in helping financial firms relocate back-office operations to the outer boroughs instead of New Jersey, Florida, Delaware, or South Dakota. Goldman Sachs, Morgan Stanley, the Securities Association Clearinghouse, Blue Cross and Blue Shield, and the American Insurance Group have moved or are moving back-office operations to Brooklyn; Citicorp and Drexel Burnham, to Queens; and Merrill Lynch to Staten Island, all with some assistance from the city.[25]

Second, the City, through the Board of Education and with assistance from the private sector, can take measures to improve public school education throughout the city. Of course, no one would argue that improvement will come easily, rapidly, or cheaply. Nevertheless, the City cannot afford not to act on it.

In general, a major trend which should play itself out in the city's favor is the trend toward vertical and horizontal "disintegration" in parts of the financial industries. This trend, which is not unlike that found in other sectors of the nation's economy, tends to benefit large urban centers because of the resulting growing emphasis on market transactions—thus, on agglomeration economies. Unfortunately, while New York may provide a fertile environment for new entrepreneurship to blossom, it fares poorly in sustaining new firms. There are many reasons, ranging from high rents to a lack of support from commercial banks or from the local bureaucracy. If the trend toward "disintegration" continues, the City will have to learn to do a better job. Failure to do so would make it that much more attractive for the industry to reorganize strong market centers elsewhere.

Notes

1. U.S. Department of Labor, Bureau of Labor Statistics, New York Region.
2. "Japanese on Wall Street," April 1988, pp. 16 and forward.
3. Perhaps the most raucous expansion drive in recent months has been that of Banca Commerciale Italiana, Italy's third largest commercial bank, in which the bank has attempted to derail Bank of New York's attempts to take-over Irving Trust to its own benefit, thus far successfully.
4. *The Future of Financial Service Industries in New York State*, The Governor's Advisory Panel on Financial Services, Chapter 1, March 1988 (draft).
5. See Richard M. Levich and Ingo Walter, Chapter 4, in this volume.
6. See Roy C. Smith, Chapter 2, in this volume.
7. Roy C. Smith, "The Eurobond Market," Working Paper #87-87, New York University, Graduate School of Business Administration, September 1987; Statistics Bureau, *Japan Statistical Yearbook 1986*, Japan Printing Bureau, 1987.
8. "Learning to Manage: A Survey of the City of London," *The Economist*, June 25, 1988; also see Steve Lohr, "Tough Securities Laws for a Wary London," *New York Times*, April 29, 1988, p. D1.
9. See Levich and Walter, Chapter 4, in this volume.
10. "Japanese on Wall Street."
11. For a discussion of this issue, see Robert Cohen, Chapter 3, in this volume.
12. "A Survey of International Banking," *The Economist*, March 26, 1988.
13. "Riding Cross-currents in Swaps," *Euromoney*, September 1987.

14. *Business Week*, May 23, 1988.

15. "Swooping in Swaps," *Euromoney*, April 1988.

16. See Levich and Walter, Chapter 4, in this volume.

17. Olivier Bertrand and Thierry Noyelle, *Human Resources and Corporate Strategy: Technological Change in Banks and Insurance Companies of Five OECD Countries* (Paris: OECD, 1988).

18. Unpublished estimates announced at Bureau of Labor Statistics Press Conference, April 1988.

19. Estimates from the Mendik Company.

20. Thierry Noyelle and Anna Dutka, *International Trade in Business Services: Accounting, Advertising, Law and Management Consulting* (Cambridge, Mass.: Ballinger, 1988).

21. Based on Noyelle and Peace's ongoing research on the development of the software industry in New York City.

22. Stephen Labaton, "Now, Global Law Firms, as U.S. Skills Are Sought," *New York Times*, May 12, 1988, pp. A1 and D20.

23. James Sterngold, "John Phelan's New Game Plan," *New York Times*, June 26, 1988, Business Section, p. 1.

24. See also Cohen, Chapter 3, in this volume.

25. City of New York, Office of Corporate and Financial Services; John Lebow, "Big Insurer Will Move 2,000 Jobs to Brooklyn," *Crain's New York Business*, June 27, 1988.

6

A U.S. Perspective on Europe 1992

Dennis Weatherstone

We are used to assuming that competition for New York emanates principally from London or Tokyo. Developments in those two cities no doubt will affect New York's financial markets for as long as we can foresee. In this chapter, however, I would like to address stirrings on the Continent that go by the shorthand of "Europe 1992" and that may generate significant new pressures for change in New York.

Europe 1992

First, a few facts. Europe 1992 refers to the deadline of December 31, 1992 that the European Community (EC) has set for itself in removing the barriers to an integrated internal market for goods and services—an objective that will have far-reaching implications. For Europe's financial markets—a comparatively small slice of the enormous sphere that will be affected—integration will mean a number of changes, including the freedom for banks and securities firms to branch and sell financial services across national borders; an end to capital controls; the elimination of taxes and regulations that discriminate against residents of the member countries; and progress toward a common supervisory standard for financial firms.

It is entirely proper to be skeptical that EC-member states will follow through on all of the pending reforms. Nevertheless, it is likely that, by 1992, Europe will have a more integrated and less regulated financial market than it has today.

As far as we can see, "1992" will have a powerful impact on Europe's retail banking, insurance, and securities markets. The prices of financial services are expected to drop dramatically as financial firms expand across borders to take advantage of a newly integrated market of 320 million people. A recent study commissioned by the EC forecasts that retail financial service prices will drop by as much as 10 percent in the European Community as a whole.[1]

In some countries the decline is expected to be even greater. In Spain, for example, protection from foreign competition has meant high profits for Spanish banks and high prices for consumers of financial services. Last year, while major banks in New York and London suffered large losses, profits at Spanish banks rose a resounding 29 percent. Such profits will most likely fall if the European market becomes truly integrated. That, of course, means that the prices of financial services in Spain will fall as well—by as much as 21 percent, according to the same EC study.

As European markets become more integrated, one might expect banking and securities business to further gravitate toward a single location, such as London, as it has done in the past. But this precedent is unlikely to hold. Financial business flocked to London in the past mainly because London was blessed with freedom from a variety of regulations and taxes that hampered the growth of business on the Continent—and in New York. Obviously, a concentration of financial expertise in London also helped. In the past few years, however, France, Italy, the Netherlands, and Spain have all liberalized their capital markets in an effort to repatriate business that had migrated abroad. Banks and securities firms in each of these countries have a natural advantage over their London-based brethren because they are close to home-currency borrowers and investors. So, as "1992" approaches, a trend toward decentralization of wholesale financial markets may emerge, with a good deal of the business previously lost to London returning to the Continent's national financial centers.

Implications for New York

At first glance, it might seem that "1992"—whose impact will be the greatest on Europe's retail markets—will have little impact on New York. But as Europe's retail markets become more competitive, America's retail markets are likely to look more and more attractive because they are comparatively less competitive. Continued restrictions on interstate banking and on securities activities make them so. Thus, we may see increasing numbers of foreign banks—not only European, but also Japanese—choosing to expand their retail operations in the United States rather than Europe.

"1992" may also lead to more competition in the United States as it creates pressure for financial deregulation in this country. The guidelines thus far adopted by the EC will allow member states to deny entry to financial firms from countries that do not permit European firms complete access to their domestic financial markets. Significantly, the reciprocity language in the guidelines is vague, giving member states wide scope for creating mischief. Most European countries allow their financial firms to engage in a wider range of securities, insurance, and investment activities than the United States or Japan do for either foreign or domestic banks. European governments annoyed by this unequal state of affairs might well shut U.S. and Japanese financial firms out of their domestic markets. They could bar them from setting up new branches or subsidiaries within their borders until the United States or Japan saw fit to extend reciprocal courtesies. All the signals suggest that EC-member countries will not be shy about seeking reciprocity from the United States between now and 1992.

Demands for reciprocity, though sometimes distasteful, are a potent force for financial liberalization—witness the gradual opening of Tokyo's financial markets under pressure from Western governments. Canada, as you may know, has launched a campaign for reciprocity for its banks in the United States. And in May 1988, the big three Swiss banks indicated that they were prepared to open their underwriting syndicate, which dominates the market for domestic Swiss franc bond issues, under certain circumstances, to foreign banks provided that those banks' home countries grant "full reciprocity" to Swiss banks. Such a rule would exclude U.S. and Japanese banks.

Given these developments, the EC's demands for reciprocity are likely to contribute greatly to the momentum for reform of the laws governing the fractured financial services industry in the United States. So let us imagine for a moment that the barriers here between commercial and investment banking, among others, were knocked down in the United States. What would happen?

An influx of new entrants into New York's securities markets, and perhaps other financial markets, would be the most likely result. U.S. and Japanese banks would open subsidiaries to underwrite and deal in corporate securities, and so would European banks whose corporate securities activities in this country were not grandfathered by the International Banking Act of 1978. Diversified financial services countries would probably try to expand their retail banking operations, particularly those that can be linked to securities or insurance products.

Perhaps inevitably, we would get falling margins, some overinvestment, and some painful shakeouts. If history is any guide, however, borrowers and investors would enjoy the lower prices that intense competition would bring.

The impact of such competition would likely be the greatest on New York's international markets. While New York has some of the world's largest domestic financial markets, it has attracted less business from abroad than might be expected. For example, New York is second to London in foreign exchange trading volume—in part, admittedly, because of London's time-zone advantage midway between Tokyo and New York. Likewise, New York last year fell behind Tokyo in cross-border lending volume, with London remaining in the lead. New York's worst record, however, is in attracting bond business from abroad. Foreign firms and governments issued only $5.9 billion in bonds in the United States in 1987, while issuing over $120 billion in the Euromarkets.

In the end, New York may join the Continent's financial centers and bring back home some of the business lost to London over the past decade. Despite a thriving domestic bond market in New York last year, companies, governments, and international agencies still issued more than $56 billion in dollar bonds abroad, in the Euromarkets. No one would argue that London will lose all that business. But by enhancing competition and harmonizing regulations, "1992" may set in motion events that will bring about not only the return of French franc business to Paris and DM business to Frankfurt but the return of dollar business to New York, as well. That will only happen, however, if our legislators and regulators allow it to happen, by reforming our outdated laws and putting us on an equal footing with forward-thinking countries and competitors abroad.

Notes

1. Price Waterhouse International Economic Consultants, "The Cost of 'Non-Europe' in Financial Services," Study prepared for the European Commission, March 1988.

About the Contributors

Robert B. Cohen is Economic Advisor to the Director of Economic Development and Senior Economist for the Industrial Development Council, State of New York. He has researched banking issues for the Joint Economic Committee of the United States Congress, the United Nations, and private banks.

Richard M. Levich is Professor of Finance and International Business and Chairman of the International Business Program at the Graduate School of Business Administration, New York University. He is also Research Associate, National Bureau of Economic Research, Cambridge, Mass.

Thierry Noyelle is Senior Research Scholar and Associate Director of the Conservation of Human Resources Project, Columbia University. His most recent book is *Human Resources and Corporate Strategy: Technological Change in Banks and Insurance Companies in Five OECD Countries* (1988).

Roy C. Smith is Professor of Finance at the Graduate School of Business Administration, New York University, and a specialist in international finance. He is a former General Partner of Goldman Sachs.

Ingo Walter is Dean Abraham L. Gitlow Professor of Economics and Finance at the Graduate School of Business Administration, New York University and John H. Loudon Professor of International Management at INSEAD, Fountainebleau, France. His most recent book is *Global Competition in Financial Services* (1988).

Dennis Weatherstone is President of J.P. Morgan & Co., Inc., and its subsidiary, Morgan Guaranty Trust Company of New York. He is a director of General Motors Corporation, Merck & Co., Inc., and a member of the New York Stock Exchange's international capital markets advisory group.

Index